MW01516952

Annabelle White's
Best
Recipes

NH
NEW
HOLLAND

ANNABELLE WHITE'S BEST RECIPES

This edition published in 1999 by New Holland Publishers (NZ) Ltd
Auckland • Sydney • London • Cape Town

218 Lake Road, Northcote, Auckland, New Zealand
14 Aquatic Drive, Frenchs Forest, NSW 2086, Australia
24 Nutford Place, London W1H 6DQ, United Kingdom
80 McKenzie Street, Cape Town 8001, South Africa

First published in 1997 by C J. Publishing
Reprinted 1998

Copyright © Text: Annabelle White
Copyright © Photography: Kieran Scott

ISBN: 1-877246-01-8

Designer/Production: **Sue Attwood**
Photographer: **Kieran Scott**
Editor: **Pamela Parsons**
Printed through **Bookbuilders Ltd,** Hong Kong

All rights reserved. No part of this publication may be reproduced, stored in
a retrieval system, or transmitted in any form or by any means, electronic,
mechanical, photocopying, recording or otherwise, without the prior
permission of the publisher.

While the publisher and author have made every effort to ensure that the
information and instructions in this book are accurate and safe, they cannot
accept liability for any resulting injury or loss or damage to property whether
direct or consequential.

Cover Photograph – Vanilla Panna Cotta
Recipe on page 90

Contents

Foreword by Alison Holst

What is the definition of a good cookbook?

To me, it is a book like this one, in which I can hear the author chatting with me as I read, sharing with me her enthusiasm and delight in the recipes she has chosen, and making me feel so excited about her ideas that I have trouble deciding whether I should read on, or rush straight away into my kitchen to prepare the food I have just read about!

There are many good cookbooks which I leave the reader to imagine what the end result looks like. Not this one! I found that the photographs were not only very decorative, but really set the mood, taking me right into the warmth of Annabelle's home to enjoy her delicious food throughout the day.

I am sure that this book will give you great pleasure as you share with Annabelle special recipes and foods which meant so much to her over the years, and which she and her talented team have presented to you so enticingly!

Good cooking.

Alison Holst

May 1997

This cookbook is dedicated to my mother, Jacqueline White, who taught me at a young age that good flavour and patience are paramount to good cooking. She firmly believes any day is enhanced by eating good food and that sitting around the table together is one of life's greatest pleasures. Every night as a family, we would sit down to a beautifully laid table and enjoy scrumptious fare. It was not just eating for sustenance – it was dining – but not in a pretentious or extravagant manner. It may have been a hearty soup, roast dinner and a fruit dessert, but it would have been perfectly cooked by her and treasured by her family.

Mum is the consummate foodie. She gets up early on the weekends and, armed with her trolley, visits the markets to collect the freshest produce and talk to the suppliers. She has a pile of cook books by her bedside, and an invitation to her dinner table is a memorable experience.

When I was 21 she wrote a cook book for me that is a gem. Brimming with culinary anecdotes and all her repertoire of great recipes, it is my most beloved possession. If there was a fire in the house, and I could only grab one thing, it would be this worn, tatty and much loved exercise book.

Introduction

As a food writer you quickly receive feedback when someone recreates your recipe and it has worked well. Their eyes seem to brighten and they become quite emotional about a particular pesto, or a scrumptious cake or a delicious stew or casserole. Their joy and their enthusiasm makes your job so worthwhile.

You also receive a great deal of mail from people who want another copy of a favourite recipe that was lost, "thrown out by mistake" or in some cases, devoured by the cat! There are always a few recipes that are consistently requested – even years after they were first published. This recipe book is a collection of these recipes.

With stylist and great friend John Borwick's enthusiasm and the culinary passion of Rodney Greaves – we made up a team. We wanted to invite you all home for the day to enjoy the house and share our love of good food and great company. So this collection is divided up into chapters relating to the times in the day when a restorative break is needed.

Starting with breakfast in bed and finishing with supper in the cook's library, you will share the day with us and the fun of considering your dining options.

These recipes are simple, no-nonsense, family favourites. There are no over-processed foods or complicated procedures. Great flavours with minimum fuss was our philosophy.

This book is dedicated to my mother, but I have another mother who needs a special mention, as some of her recipes are in this book. When I was 17, I spent a year in Dover, Delaware in the United States as an American Field Scholar. Living with an Italian-American family, the Mestro family, for one year was an unforgettable experience. The essential core to this family is the warmth, love, laughter and exuberance around the family dinner table. This is where I was first introduced to the Mediterranean table – eating sensational pasta, homemade sauces, great Italian cheeses, meats and baked goods. This is where I first sampled zucchini (courgette), eggplant (aubergine), fresh basil and bell peppers (capsicums).

Every Sunday morning the smell of the tomato ragù on the stove and the cosy aroma of fresh apple cake was our wake-up call. Bettie Mestro worked incredibly demanding hours during the week and when she was home, she was cooking. It was a labour of love for her family, and her kitchen is one of my favourite places to be.

My American father, Bill Mestro, is in the supermarket business, so his quest for excellent products to sell always transfers to serving the best at home. As an addition to the family, your appreciation of flavour and quality was their greatest reward.

Flavour was a paramount goal when working on this cook book, and it had to be personal. Photographed in my own home, not in a studio. I live on the sunny side of a hill, with most of my house circled by bush. The native bird chorus wakes you up, the house is always full of wondrous smells and when you come to visit I have a compulsion to feed you and send you home with the leftovers.

The cedar house is best described as an "upmarket tramper's hut". I wanted visitors to feel the same sense of delight you do when walking through the bush and finally see the hut after a day of hard walking.

It's my beloved home, but it's also the location for entertaining, reading, writing, developing recipes, and researching food trends. We hope we have captured this all on film.

So this book is a personal invitation into my home, coupled with the best recipes I have developed in the last eight years as a food writer. This collection also includes other cook's recipes that I have sampled, made at home and truly enjoy.

The recipes are stylish but simple, and every one is achievable without breaking your budget. And, most important of all, our book is user-friendly.

Welcome home and I hope you have a delicious stay!

Anabelle White

BIRKENHEAD POINT

Breakfast in Bed

"Life, within doors, has few pleasanter prospects
than a neatly arranged and well provisioned
breakfast-table"

NATHANIEL HAWTHORNE

The House of the Seven Gables

With the early morning bird chorus and the
distinctive fresh smell of the bush – getting up
from your slumbers is never easier.

Fruit Smoothies

A fruit smoothie is a heroic start to a brunch.

FOR YOUR SMOOTHIE: Purée one banana in a blender with a few slices of fresh pawpaw, add 150 g plain yoghurt, a heaped tablespoon wheat germ and thin with orange juice. Garnish with mint.

OTHER SMOOTHIE SUGGESTIONS: orange and banana, yoghurt and orange juice or strawberries, yoghurt and apple juice. Let your imagination go crazy and combine fresh fruit, yoghurt and juice in new ways as a basis for this creamy and palatable breakfast food.

Fresh Berry Kir Imperial

Combining fruit and bubbles makes an extra special breakfast.

3 cups fresh ripe berries – raspberries are ideal – plus more for garnish
1 bottle methode traditionelle or champagne
1½ cups fresh blueberries – plus more for garnish

Put 8 champagne flutes in the freezer. Put 1½ cups raspberries and 6 tablespoons of bubbly in a blender and purée till smooth.

Remove the glasses from the freezer. Divide the remaining berries between the glasses – then pour some of the raspberry purée over the fruit. Top with champagne.

Garnish with extra berries, if desired.

TO MAKE YOUR BREAKFAST MEMORABLE

• Serve cheese at room temperature with heated bagels or rolls.

• Use produce from your own back yard. If you have a bumper harvest of plums – make a stunning fresh fruit Muesli fruit cobbler for breakfast. Place a kilo of sliced plums in a large oven-proof dish with 3 tablespoons water. In the food processor whirl 1 cup of your favourite toasted cereal for a minute, add 4 tablespoons softened butter, process again. Place this "ball" in a bowl and with your hands combine another cup of toasted muesli. Scatter this over the plums and bake 30 minutes on 160°C. Serve warm, not hot, with plain yoghurt.

• Always make sure you search out a good coffee supplier and have fresh orange juice in the fridge as well as extra bottles of bubbly.

Fruit Smoothie

Easy Bran Muffins

The great feature of this recipe is that you make the mix in advance and leave it in the fridge. In the morning you simply grease some muffin pans and bake them while you shower or fix breakfast for the family.

The mixture will keep up to a week in the fridge and is a wonderful stand-by over a long weekend if unexpected visitors arrive for breakfast or coffee.

Makes 24-30

3 cups bran

1 cup boiling water

2 large lightly beaten eggs

1 cup yoghurt

1 cup milk

½ cup salad oil or ½ cup melted butter

1 cup sultanas or 1 cup raisins

½ cup finely chopped apricots

¼ cup chopped walnuts (optional)

2½ teaspoons baking soda

½ teaspoon salt

½ cup brown sugar

1½ cups flour

1 cup wholemeal flour

In a large bowl mix bran with boiling water. Set aside until cool, then add eggs, yoghurt, milk, salad oil/ melted butter, sultanas/ raisins, apricots and walnuts.

In a separate bowl, stir together baking soda, salt, sugar and flours. Blend thoroughly and stir into bran mixture.

To store, refrigerate batter in tightly covered container for up to one week.

Bake at 220°C for 15-20 minutes.

You can also add a mashed banana to this mixture with the other dried fruit. Obviously any mix of dried fruit making up a generous cup will work as well. Also if you have a container of buttermilk in your fridge you can add 2 cups of buttermilk instead of the milk/ yoghurt combination.

Fresh Fruit Salad

Fresh fruit salad is always popular and, like a fruit smoothie, is only limited by your imagination. You can make up a fruit syrup like this or simply pour a little orange juice with finely chopped mint over your bowl of fruit.

Serves 4

¼ cup caster sugar

¾ cup water

1 orange, peeled & sliced horizontally

2 cups seedless grapes

½ punnet strawberries

1 mango or pawpaw

juice of ½ orange

Put the sugar and water into a heavy saucepan. Stir over gentle heat until the sugar has dissolved, then raise the heat and bring the syrup to the boil without stirring. Boil the syrup hard for 2 to 3 minutes, then remove from the heat and cool the syrup by placing the saucepan in a sink of iced water.

While the syrup cools, prepare the fruit. Pour the cold syrup over the fruit, add the orange juice and serve at room temperature – preferably in a glass bowl.

Fresh Fruit Salad

Apricot Cinnamon Muffins

These stunning muffins can be made with any fruit, and the aroma of sweet cinnamon and sugar baking in the house inspires any cook. Don't expect any leftovers, but you can freeze them and reheat later if desired.

2 cups flour
4 teaspoons baking powder
½ cup sugar
1 heaped teaspoon cinnamon
1 cup sliced dried apricots
1 large egg
½ cup milk
½ cup cream
¼ cup oil

Place the dry ingredients with the dried apricots in a bowl. In another bowl beat the egg with the milk/cream and oil. Add to the dried ingredients gently. Do not over-mix. Place in well greased muffin pans. Bake 200°C for 15 minutes.

NOTE: You do not need to use cream in this recipe – you can use all milk instead. You can also use buttermilk instead of cream if you are trying to clean up supplies from the fridge.

Zachary's Buttermilk Pancakes

My nephew Zachary (4) loves pancakes and his idea of fun is for all the family to gather around and consume a short stack of pancakes each. With pure maple syrup and all the laughter – breakfast should be like this every day.

2 large eggs
¼ cup vegetable oil or melted butter
½ teaspoon grated lemon zest
1 cup buttermilk
2 tablespoons brown sugar
2 teaspoons baking powder
½ teaspoon baking soda
½ teaspoon salt
1½ cups flour

Beat eggs in a large bowl; beat in the remaining ingredients in order, mixing until smooth. For each pancake, pour about ¼ cup batter on to a hot greased griddle or fry pan. Turn the pancakes when the tops are covered with bubbles and cook the other side. Serve with syrup or hot jam.

NOTE: We added 1 cup fresh blueberries to this recipe just prior to cooking. These pancakes are also delicious served with orange butter.

Orange Butter

125 g butter
2 tablespoons brown sugar
3 teaspoons finely grated orange rind
4 tablespoons fresh orange juice

Cream the butter, sugar and orange rind. Beat in the orange juice, 1 tablespoon at a time, until light and fluffy. Store in the refrigerator and bring to room temperature before serving.

Zachary's Blueberry Buttermilk Pancakes

Smoked Hoki and Kumara Fishcakes

This recipe was developed by Wellington chef Al Brown and was first printed in 1994. Like all his great food, it's simple and not overworked. One of the staff at my local post office stopped me recently and said these fish cakes were her family's favourite dish.

Serves 4

olive oil for cooking
600 g smoked Hoki fish fillets
2 cups milk
olive oil for cooking
2 cups finely chopped onion
1 finely chopped green capsicum
¼ cup finely chopped celery
1½ tablespoons garlic
1 tablespoon dried thyme
1 large kumara diced
1 cup mayonnaise
3 tablespoons lemon juice
1 cup fresh breadcrumbs

Remove skin from the smoked hoki fillets. Place in a saucepan, cover with milk and poach for 5 minutes. Remove from heat and strain off milk.

In a sauté pan on moderate heat add a small amount of olive oil. Add chopped onions, capsicum, celery, garlic and dried thyme. Lower heat and cook until all vegetables are soft. Remove from pan and cool.

In a separate pot, cook the kumara in salted cold water. Remove and strain as soon as the water begins to boil. Cool.

Take a large mixing bowl and mix all the cooked ingredients. Add the mayonnaise and lemon juice. Season with salt and pepper. Finally, fold in the breadcrumbs until the mixture is firm and easily moulded into cakes.

Heat a sauté pan to moderate to high heat. Add a small amount of olive oil. Take the moulded fish cakes, place in pan and cook until golden brown on both sides and heated through. Remove and keep in a warm place.

....

NOTE: We served these fish cakes with a soft-boiled egg, but you can garnish with red capsicum and chervil or parsley. Serving these cakes with garlic prawns and a jalapeño tartare sauce makes a great entrée or lunch dish.

Irish Potato Cakes

Everyone loves potatoes! Whenever I broadcast or print a potato recipe, the response is always overwhelming.

1 medium, raw potato, grated
1 cup cooked mashed potato
½ cup self-raising flour
½ teaspoon baking soda
½ teaspoon nutmeg
1 teaspoon vinegar
¾ cup milk
2 tablespoons melted butter

Squeeze grated raw potato to remove excess liquid and combine with cooked potato, self-raising flour, baking soda and nutmeg.

Stir vinegar into milk and allow to stand for 2 minutes. Add milk and butter to potato mixture.

Stir gently until well combined.

Drop spoonfuls of mixture onto well-greased pan. Cook on both sides until golden brown and cooked through.

....

NOTE: Delicious with smoked salmon, scrambled eggs flecked with parsley and even cold meat for dinner.

Smoked Hoki and Kumara Fishcakes

Chicken and Feta Fritters

Everyone loves fritters and these are superb. They are a great means of using up left-over ham or poultry. Serve with a fresh zingy salsa and the full savoury notes of the slow-baked tomatoes.

Serves 4

4 medium potatoes
2 tablespoons lemon juice
150 g feta, crumbled
200 g cooked diced chicken, bones and skin removed
4 spring onions – tops, finely sliced
2 teaspoons freshly chopped coriander
¼ cup flour
2 large eggs, lightly beaten
salt and freshly ground black pepper to taste
olive oil for cooking

Cook the unpeeled potatoes until they are still firm. Drain, cool and peel. Grate the potatoes. Place in a bowl with the next five ingredients. Sprinkle the flour over the top and blend through gently. Add eggs and seasoning and mix well.

Cook the fritters in olive oil till golden brown on each side. Allow about 3-4 minutes per side. Remove, place on paper towels and keep warm in the oven. Serve with mango mint salsa and slow-baked tomatoes.

NOTE: When cooking fritters keep the pan hot and use a liberal amount of cooking oil. Rather than soaking up the oil, the extra oil and high heat actually will produce a crispy fritter.

Mango Mint Salsa

½ ripe mango, peeled, seeded and diced
2 tablespoons finely chopped fresh mint
1 tablespoon fresh lime juice
⅛ teaspoon salt
A generous splash of jalapeño sauce (optional)
½ spring onion, finely diced

Combine all the ingredients in a bowl. Adjust the salt and lime juice to taste.

NOTE: Jalapeño sauce is available from the gourmet section of the supermarket and is one of my favourite condiments. To really appreciate the impact jalapeño sauce has on food, simply add a few generous splashes to diced avocado with a little minced red onion. Add a little chopped coriander and hide the sauce in the cupboard so you can eat the lot!

Slow-baked Tomatoes

5 tablespoons peanut oil
8 medium tomatoes
2 teaspoons sugar
½ teaspoon salt
½ teaspoon freshly ground black pepper
3 medium cloves garlic, minced
1 tablespoon olive oil
½ cup minced fresh parsley

Preheat the oven to 150°C. Spread the oil in a lamington tin. Cut off one-third of the stem end of the tomatoes. Discard the cut-off ends. Place the tomatoes in the pan, cut side down, and bake for 30 minutes. Turn and bake for another 30 minutes, basting with the pan juices occasionally. Sprinkle with the sugar, salt and pepper. Cook for another 1½ hours until tomatoes are flattened.

Sauté the garlic in the olive oil over medium heat until soft, about 4 minutes. Do not brown. Stir parsley and sprinkle over cooked tomatoes.

Slow-baked Tomatoes

Salmon Cakes

Don't just serve these at breakfast – they are equally good with a mixed green salad for lunch.

750 g salmon fillet, skinned
6 finely chopped spring onions
2 tablespoons fresh minced ginger
3 large eggs, lightly beaten
2 tablespoons cornflour
1 tablespoon fresh lemon juice
1 tablespoon soy sauce
salt and pepper to taste
¼ cup vegetable oil (more if necessary)

Preheat oven to 100°C. Chop the salmon coarsely with a knife (using a food processor will give the cakes a mealy texture). In a large bowl, mix the salmon with the remaining ingredients except the oil. Shape in 12 patties and set aside. When ready to cook them, heat 1 tablespoon of vegetable oil in a large nonstick pan. Cook a batch at a time and sauté the cakes until lightly browned on both sides – about 3 minutes.

Add oil to pan as needed. Drain cakes on paper towels. Transfer to a heatproof platter and keep warm in oven for up to 30 minutes.

....

NOTE: Serve with softly scrambled eggs.

Corn Fritters with Bacon and Tomatoes

A universal favourite – add a little chilli to this recipe for extra heat if you prefer a kick-start to the morning. This recipe has been adapted from a recipe given to me by New Zealand chef Peter Gordon of The Sugar Club in London.

For 6 good-sized fritters

4 fresh ears of corn
4 large eggs
½ cup sour cream
¼ cup cornmeal
¼ cup cornflour
1 teaspoon salt
1 teaspoon freshly cracked black pepper
½ cup finely sliced chives

Cut the kernels of corn off the cob, being extremely careful as knives can often slip on such jobs. Whisk the eggs with the sour cream, then mix all the remaining ingredients, including the corn, together. Fry in butter or cooking oil in a moderately hot frying pan until golden on the bottom and firm on the top. Flip over and cook until done. Best eaten hot, but good eaten cold.

....

NOTE: Serve like a hamburger with cooked bacon and tomatoes and garnish with fresh herbs.

For another stunning combination, serve with smoked salmon and a little extra sour cream.

Corn Fritters with Bacon and Tomatoes

Banana Tea Bread

A great way to use up extra-ripe fruit from the fruit bowl. You can also toast this under the grill for breakfast!

1½ cups self-raising flour

¼ teaspoon soda

½ teaspoon salt

85 g butter

⅔ cup sugar

2 large eggs, beaten

2 or 3 bananas peeled and mashed

125 g walnuts, coarsely chopped

Grease a loaf tin. Sift the flour, soda and salt. Cream the butter and sugar, add eggs and beat well. Add bananas and beat again. Stir in the flour and nuts and bake 180°C for 60 minutes or until risen and just firm. You can prepare this the day before and it will still taste fresh baked!

....

NOTE: If you use three bananas, the loaf will be very moist and can be served warm with cream as a dessert.

Sour Cream Coffee Cake

Another breakfast classic – this is a delicious cake and the ingredients are easily found. Serve with lashings of good coffee.

125 g butter, softened

1 cup sugar

2 large eggs

1 teaspoon vanilla

1 cup sour cream

1 teaspoon baking soda

2 cups flour

¼ teaspoon salt

1½ teaspoons baking powder

¼ cup chopped nuts

¼ cup brown sugar

1 teaspoon cinnamon

Cream the butter and sugar until light and fluffy. Add the eggs and vanilla and mix well. Stir in the sour cream and the soda, mix well. Mix the flour, salt and baking powder and fold gently into the sour-cream mixture. Do not beat.

Place half the mixture in a well-greased 22 cm ring tin. Mix the nuts, brown sugar and cinnamon and spoon half on batter in pan. Place remaining cake mixture over the nuts. Sprinkle the remaining nut mix on top of the cake.

Bake at 180°C for 45 minutes or until an inserted cake tester comes out clean. Let stand for five minutes before inverting onto a plate.

Sour Cream
Coffee Cake

Morning Coffee in the Bush

When the mid-morning sun streams through the bush, morning coffee seems a grand idea. The aroma of roasted beans, coupled with fresh baking, creates a cosy and inviting opportunity to pause and appreciate a moment of morning quiet. If only glorious mid-morning light could last all day!

Apricot and Prune Cake

This is my favourite cake for morning coffee. I published it years ago and constantly receive mail from readers wanting the recipe again. Once you make it and try it – it becomes a regularly baked item. One reader said her husband would utter sounds of great delight whenever he saw the apricots and prunes being placed on the bench!

¾ cup chopped dried apricots

¾ cup chopped pitted prunes

water or cold tea

170 g butter

¾ cup sugar

2 large eggs

2 cups flour

½ teaspoon salt

2 teaspoons baking powder

½ cup milk

Cover the chopped apricots and prunes with water or cold, strained tea. Leave for a few hours.

Cream the butter and the sugar until light and fluffy. Add the eggs, dried ingredients and milk.

Lastly, add drained fruit.

Mix separately: ½ cup brown sugar, 1 tablespoon flour and 1 tablespoon cinnamon.

Place one-third of the batter in a greased 25 cm ring tin, sprinkle with a third of the brown sugar mixture and repeat twice.

Bake at 170°C for 45-60 minutes or until a skewer comes clean when tested.

....

NOTE: This cake can be served with whipped cream and a dash of brandy.

Favourite Chocolate Cake

When I was a child my mother would make this cake whenever the Rotarians came for committee meeting suppers. I'm sure this cake was an incentive. Early the next day, my sister and I would search the fridge for leftovers. Delicious iced with chocolate icing and garnished with walnuts.

130 g butter

3 tablespoons cocoa

¾ cup water

5 large eggs, at room temperature

1¼ cup sugar

1¾ cups flour

1½ teaspoon cream of tartar

¾ teaspoon baking soda

Filling:

raspberry jam

whipped cream

icing sugar

Boil together the butter, cocoa, and water. Beat eggs until thick, then add the sugar gradually, beating well. Fold in the sifted dry ingredients, then add the boiling chocolate mixture.

Pour into a 23 cm greased and floured cake tin. Bake at 180°C for 45 minutes or until a knife comes out cleanly. Cool, split in half, spread each half with jam, then sandwich with whipped cream. Dust with icing sugar.

Dutch Ginger Slice

Visiting *Café Replete* in Taupo several years ago I noticed people lining up for this slice. It's so simple and just superb with lots of coffee.

400 g butter
225 g ginger in syrup
3 eggs
4 cups flour
2 – 2½ cups white sugar
35 g (½ a 70 g packet of raw sliced almonds)

Melt the butter in a large bowl in the microwave. Cut the ginger into smaller pieces and place in the food processor. Process until it forms a thick paste. Add this to the melted butter and then allow to cool a little. Add the beaten eggs and the flour and sugar.

Place the mixture into a well-greased 28 cm x 44 cm baking tray. Sprinkle the sliced almonds over the mixture and bake until golden, about 35-40 minutes at 180°C. Cut each tray into 20 slices before completely cooled.

....

NOTE: You can double this recipe successfully. For two baking trays: 800 g butter, 8 cups flour, 5 cups white sugar, 5 eggs, 450 g ginger in syrup and the whole packet of raw sliced almonds.

Ginger Cake

My mother has made this cake for years. Please note there are no eggs in this recipe.

2½ cups flour
2 teaspoons ground ginger
1 teaspoon cinnamon
1 teaspoon mixed spice
3 tablespoons golden syrup
1 cup milk
125 g butter
1¼ cups sugar
3 teaspoon baking soda

Sift the flour, ginger, cinnamon and mixed spice into a bowl. Warm the golden syrup, milk, butter and sugar together.

Stir in soda and cool to lukewarm. Mix in dry ingredients. Bake while mixture is still warm at 180°C for about 45 minutes in a 20 cm tin. Ice with a plain icing. It's also delicious sliced and buttered.

Dutch Ginger Slice

Rhubarb Muffins

Even people who dislike rhubarb love these muffins. Readers continually request this recipe, and their feed-back has been inspiring. Good news if you have rhubarb in the garden! Since buttermilk has an extended shelf life in the fridge, you can easily make batch after batch of these delectable goodies without making extra trips to the shops.

Makes 12

1¼ cups brown sugar

½ cup salad oil

1 large egg

2 teaspoons vanilla essence

1 cup buttermilk (or ¾ cup yoghurt
    with ⅓ cup milk)

1½ cups rhubarb, finely chopped
    (select nice thin stems)

½ cup chopped walnuts

2½ cups flour

1 teaspoon baking powder

pinch of salt

Topping:
2 teaspoons ground
cinnamon
1 tablespoon melted
    butter
⅓ cup sugar

Grease muffin tin. Preheat oven to 200°C. Combine the brown sugar, oil, egg, vanilla essence and buttermilk in a large bowl. Mix well. Stir in the rhubarb and the walnuts. In a separate bowl mix the flour, baking powder and salt. Lightly blend these dry ingredients into the rhubarb mixture. Fill muffin tins to ⅔ full. Combine topping ingredients and sprinkle over muffins. Bake 20-25 minutes.

Orange and Date Muffins

A very moist and full-flavoured muffin. The aroma while the muffins are cooking is just sensational!

Makes 24

2 oranges

2 large eggs

200 g melted butter

1 cup dates (roughly chopped)

400 g plain yoghurt (with a little lemon
    juice added)

¾ sugar

3 cups flour

2 teaspoon soda

2 teaspoon baking powder

½ teaspoon salt

Preheat the oven to 200°C.
Blend the whole oranges in the food processor – skin, seeds – everything! Add eggs and melted butter (cooled slightly) and whirl the mixture all around, but don't over-process.

Place in a large bowl and add dates. Mix the yoghurt and sugar together in a jug or bowl. Sift the dry ingredients into another bowl.

Alternately add the yoghurt mixture and the dry ingredients and just blend, do not over-mix.

Place in greased muffin pans and bake at 200°C for 15-20 minutes.

NOTE: These muffins keep well for up to three days. If your pantry is low on dates, you can use figs or raisins.

Cinnamon Biscuits

This recipe comes from Prue and David at *Vinnies* – a fine restaurant in Auckland. After a stunning dinner, these biscuits were served with coffee. But these delights can be savoured anytime of the day!

Makes about 30 small biscuits.

½ cup olive oil
½ cup caster sugar
1 large egg
1½ cups flour
1 teaspoon baking powder
1 teaspoon freshly ground cinnamon
pinch of salt
50 g ground almonds

Beat the olive oil and sugar together. Add remaining ingredients and combine well. Form into two logs and wrap in plastic wrap. Freeze for 3 to 4 hours. Slice into ¾ centimetre rounds.

Bake in a 190°C oven until golden (about 10-15 minutes) – but keep an eye on them as they burn quickly.

....

NOTE: Take a couple of minutes to grind a cinnamon stick in a spice mill or mortar – that aroma of freshly ground cinnamon is irresistible! Keep unbaked mixture in the freezer for next time; just thaw slightly, slice and bake.

Toasted Pine Nut Biscuits

125 g butter
½ cup brown sugar
½ cup white sugar
1 teaspoon vanilla
1 large egg
1-1¼ cups flour
½ teaspoon baking powder
½ cup lightly toasted pine nuts
additional toasted pine nuts
icing sugar for garnish

Cream the butter and sugar. Add vanilla and egg. Slowly incorporate the flour and baking powder. Carefully stir in the toasted pine nuts.

Drop teaspoons of the batter about 2.5 cm apart on 2 greased baking trays.

Bake at 190°C until light brown or about 10 minutes. Halfway through the cooking, add a few additional toasted pine nuts for garnish.

Place on a cooling rack until room temperature. Sprinkle with icing sugar; if desired.

These biscuits are best eaten the day they are made.

Toasted Pine Nut Biscuits

Cheese and Bacon Muffins

A great way to use leftovers: 1 to 2 tablespoons of sweet corn, a few chopped mushrooms, even a little grated carrot or courgette. Don't add too much or the muffins will be soggy. Great for morning tea, this recipe can also be made into mini muffins for cocktail nibbles. Just split open and place a slice of brie in the muffin, reheat gently and when the brie begins to melt, remove from the oven and serve.

Makes 6

1 cup grated cheddar cheese
$\frac{1}{3}$ cup bacon or ham, chopped finely
$1\frac{1}{2}$ cups flour
1 tablespoon baking powder
ground black pepper
1 large egg, lightly beaten
2 tablespoons chopped fresh chives
    and/or parsley
75 g butter
1 cup milk

Grease muffin tins. Preheat the oven to 200°C. Place the cheese, bacon or ham, flour, baking powder and pepper in a large bowl and mix well. Add the egg and herbs.

Melt the butter in the milk and fold into dry ingredients. Spoon mixture into prepared muffin tins and top with extra grated cheese.

Bake for 15 to 20 minutes.

Blueberry and Raspberry Muffins

Each year on January 2 these muffins bursting with fruit are my birthday present to a good friend. It's an annual tradition and not to be missed. I created these muffins about 10 years ago to make something special for a boating trip. With the dry salt conditions of the wind and sea spray, I wanted something easy to eat with so much fruit flavour and sweetness exploding in your mouth it would be refreshing.

Makes 12

125 g butter
125 g sugar
2 large eggs
2 cups flour
1 heaped teaspoon baking powder
$\frac{1}{2}$ cup milk
1 cup frozen berries ($\frac{1}{2}$ cup each blueberries
    and raspberries)

Butter your muffin tins. Preheat the oven to 200°C. Cream the butter and sugar until pale and fluffy. Add eggs, beating well. Adding a little flour will stop the mixture from curdling.

Sift the flour and baking powder and add to the creamed mixture with the milk. Fold in the berries - the mixture will be stiff.

Spoon into prepared muffin tins and bake 15 minutes or until the tops are springy.

Let cool slightly before turning out of the tins. To serve, sift icing sugar over tops.

These muffins have a cake consistency and do not need buttering.

....

NOTE: Great to take when visiting friends – wrap muffins in a tea towel and place in a basket. They are ideal when warm and with plenty of fresh coffee.

Apricot Streusel Tartlets

Years ago when I taught English and History full-time, colleagues who loved good coffee would suggest visiting a local café for lunch. Apricot tarts, similar to these, were always a highlight.

100 g dried apricots
hot water
⅓ cup sugar
1 tablespoon self-raising flour
¾ cup sour cream
1 large egg
6 unbaked sweet short pastry tartlet cases (10 cm)

Topping:
30 g butter
¼ cup sugar
½ cup finely blanched almonds
½ teaspoon cinnamon

Chop the apricots, cover with hot water, stand 1 hour; drain.

Combine sugar and sifted flour, sour cream and egg, stir until well blended. Stir in apricots; fill into tartlet cases.

FOR TOPPING: Cut butter into small pieces. Combine remaining ingredients in bowl. Add butter and rub into dry ingredients until mixture is crumbly.

Sprinkle topping over tartlets; bake at 180°C for 15-25 minutes or until light golden brown.

Fresh Apple Cake

This is a great cake – when I make it for chefs they often ask for the recipe. The advantage of this cake is that you can make it in the tin in which you bake it! Quick and easy clean-up guaranteed!

125 g butter
3 cups grated peeled apple
1 cup brown sugar
1 large egg
2 cups flour
1 teaspoon baking soda
1 teaspoon mixed spice
1 teaspoon cinnamon
½ teaspoon ground nutmeg
½ teaspoon salt
1 cup sultanas
½ cup chopped walnuts

Butter generously the inside of a 25 cm cake tin. If you are careful with the mixing, a loose-bottomed tin will do. Melt the butter and let it cool. Peel and grate the apples by hand or you can grate them in the food processor.

Put them into the bottom of the greased tin, and sprinkle the brown sugar over them. Then place the cooled butter on top. Mix well with a fork. Add egg. Mix well. Sift in the flour, soda, spices and salt. Stir again. Add dried fruit and nuts. Bake at 180°C for 45-60 minutes. Test with a knife and if it does not come clean – cook for a little longer.

NOTE: This cake also proves to be a popular and easy dessert. Just serve with a scoop of vanilla ice cream. Leftovers the next day taste just as good.

Apricot Streusel Tartlets

Date and Lime Cake

100 g butter

100 g sugar

75 g brown sugar

2 large eggs lightly beaten

1½ cups flour

2 teaspoons baking soda

1 lime

1 cup stoned dates

1 cup sour cream

Icing:

3 tablespoons butter

2 cups icing sugar

3 tablespoons sour cream

½ teaspoon vanilla essence

1 teaspoon lime juice, or more according
    to taste

FOR THE CAKE: Cream the butter and sugars until light and fluffy. Gradually add the lightly beaten eggs, beating well after each addition. Sift the flour and baking soda into another bowl.

Cut 1 lime into halves, remove any seeds. Chop and grind in a blender or food processor together with the dates. (Yes, you read correctly. The whole lime minus the seeds is used in this recipe.) Add the lime and date mixture to the creamed butter.

Add the flour and soda alternately with the sour cream.

Place in a greased 23 cm ring tin and bake at 180°C for 35 minutes or until a knife comes clean when tested.

FOR THE ICING: Cream the butter, add the other ingredients and beat well together.

....

NOTE: If you don't have a lime in the kitchen, you can use a fresh lemon.

You can serve this cake without the icing if you prefer.

Kelly's Fresh Peach Cake

When a special visitor comes for morning tea, it's fun to personalise the food around that person. My brother Kelly loves peaches, and one day this cake was created in his honour. The fabulous feature of this cake is that you can use any stone fruit.

190 g softened butter

1 cup sugar

3 large eggs

3 cups fresh peaches, peeled and sliced thinly

¾ cup yoghurt

¾ cup walnuts, chopped

juice of ½ lemon

2 teaspoons grated lemon rind

2 cups flour

2 heaped teaspoons baking powder

Cream the softened butter with the sugar. When the mixture is light and creamy, add the eggs and beat well. Add the peaches, yoghurt, walnuts, lemon juice and rind. Sift the flour and the baking powder together and blend into the peach mixture. Take care not to over-mix.

Bake in a greased 20 cm cake tin at 180°C for 45 to 60 minutes.

Date and
Lime Cake

Lunch on the Terrace

Lunch on the terrace should be this easy.
Picture pleasant company gathered around the
table with good wine and a stunningly presented
antipasti plate. Add a basket of good bread and a
fruit finale and lunch never was so simple or so
much fun...

Antipasto

Antipasto literally means "before pasta". This Italian term refers to hot and cold colourful vegetables, golden cheeses, sausage and full-flavoured olives, chewy sun-dried tomatoes and strips of roasted capsicums arranged on a large platter. Piled with crunchy vegetables, rich cheeses and sausages with a distinctively fresh aroma – the antipasto platter is versatile and appealing. Keep it super fresh and super simple and the results will delight you.

To make a stunning antipasto platter, we used Portuguese chorizo*, bocconcini**, sun-dried capsicums and marinated, raw, wafer-thin slices of courgette with olives and feta on this large platter.

Meatballs (veal, chicken or lamb with olives) and bruschetta topped with tapenade*** or pesto and fresh herbs are also delicious additions to antipasto. Try this suggestion:

Warm Green Bean Salad

500 g small string beans, tipped and stemmed
3 anchovies, diced
1 heaped teaspoon Dijon mustard
salt to taste and freshly ground black pepper
2 tablespoons balsamic vinegar
5 tablespoons extra-virgin olive oil
3-5 rashers bacon, cut into pieces and cooked
  till crisp

Blanch the string beans in boiling water for 2 minutes. Place the anchovies in a small food processor and add the mustard and pepper. Add the vinegar and the oil very slowly, drop by drop at first, while the machine is running.

Place the warm beans and cooked bacon on a platter and pour the dressing over the top.

NOTE: Serve with crunchy bread.

Red Capsicum Pesto****

This recipe was developed by top Auckland caterer Kathy Paterson.

4 red capsicums, roasted and skinned
½ cup cashew nuts, toasted
3 cloves garlic, crushed
¼ cup olive oil
salt to taste

Process together the capsicums, cashew nuts and garlic, then drizzle in the oil.

Serve with Lebanese crisps.

Lebanese crisps

Cut and split the Lebanese bread into 4 pieces.

Brush with olive oil, sprinkle with sesame seeds, then cut into pieces.

Toast in the oven 190°C until golden brown. (Watch them as they only need a few minutes!)

* A type of pork sausage.

** Balls of Mozzarella cheese sometimes packed in whey.

*** Tapenade is a thick paste of capers, anchovies, black olives, olive oil, lemon juice, seasonings and occasionally tuna. From Provence.

**** A pesto is a rich oily sauce made with herbs, garlic, pine nuts, basil and cheese.

Antipasto Platter

Eggplant and Tunisian Lamb with Harissa

Harissa is a North African relish. Locals usually use just finely ground red chillies. I've tamed it down with red capsicums. Harissa is to the North Africans as pesto is to the Italians.

Tomato Harissa:
2 large red capsicums
2 cloves garlic, finely chopped
2 tablespoons ground coriander
2 tablespoons ground toasted caraway seeds
1 large tomato, seeded and diced
½ teaspoons salt
1-2 fresh chillies, finely chopped,
    or ¾ teaspoon cayenne pepper

Blend red capsicums to a purée in a food processor. Drain off any excess liquid and mix in all the remaining ingredients, except the chilli and salt. Season to taste with chilli and salt.

Eggplant and Tunisian Lamb Mince Cakes

1 cup minced lamb
1 clove garlic, finely
    chopped
2 tablespoons onion,
    finely chopped
1 tablespoon toasted
    sesame seeds
pinch cayene pepper
1-2 medium-sized eggplants
½ cup clarified butter
½ cup clear honey
1 tablespoon freshly
    chopped coriander
1-½ teaspoons finely
    chopped chilli
salt & pepper

Mix minced lamb with garlic, onion and sesame seeds. Season with cayenne pepper and salt. Slice eggplant into circles approximately ¾ cm thick – prepare 24 slices. Place 12 slices on a clean bench board and lightly season with salt and pepper. Place 1 tablespoon of the mince on each circle of eggplant, place the remaining slice on top of the mince and press down.

Heat some clarified butter in a large frypan until just smoking, add the eggplant cakes and sear until golden brown – approx 30 seconds each side. Add the clear honey, lower the heat and let the honey caramelise on the eggplant cakes. Turn cakes in the honey, sprinkle with fresh coriander and diced chillies and season lightly with salt and pepper.

To serve, spoon the harissa on four plates. Place 3 caramelised eggplant cakes on the harissa, garnish with fancy lettuce and grilled Mediterranean-style veges.

Kumara Soup

75 g butter
2 cloves garlic, minced
6 stalks celery, diced
2 large onions, chopped
500 g kumara
1 teaspoon curry powder
2 cups chicken stock
3 cups milk
¼ cup cream
salt and pepper
chopped chives (garnish)

Place butter in a large pan and add the minced garlic, celery and onions. Peel kumara and slice into 1 cm chunks. Add curry powder to garlic mixture, then the kumara.

Cook in butter without browning for 2 minutes. Add stock, cover and cook for 10 minutes until tender.

Purée in food processor, thin with milk and add cream. Reheat without boiling. Season.

Serve with a swirl of extra cream and chopped chives.

Pear Caponata

This relish is also delicious as a side dish.

Serves 8 as an appetiser

2 x 400 g tins peeled Italian
    plum tomatoes
1 medium eggplant
salt
6 tablespoons olive oil
2 teaspoons sugar
2 pears, peeled
1 large onion, peeled
    and chopped
2 cloves garlic, peeled
    and finely chopped
2 tablespoons drained capers
¼ cup currants
2 teaspoons balsamic vinegar
freshly ground pepper
1 baguette, sliced and toasted

Drain tomatoes, reserving juice. Chop coarsely and set aside.

Slice eggplant into 1 cm rounds. Sprinkle with salt and leave to drain for 30 minutes. Rinse well and pat dry. Cut slices into 1 cm cubes. In a bowl toss eggplant with 4 tablespoons olive oil and a teaspoon of sugar.

Cut the flesh from pears in 1 cm chunks. In a second bowl toss pears with a tablespoon of oil and tea-spoon of sugar.

Heat oven to 225°C. Place 2 medium-sized baking pans in oven for 5 minutes. Remove from oven and spread eggplant in one and pears in the other.

Return to oven; roast for 25 minutes, or until eggplant and pears are tender and golden brown, shaking pans after 15 minutes.

Meanwhile, in a large sauté pan, heat the remaining 1 tablespoon olive oil over medium heat. Add onion and garlic; cook until golden, about 7 minutes. Add eggplant, tomatoes, ⅔ cup reserved tomato juice and capers. Cook over medium-low heat for 10 minutes, stirring occasionally. Add pears and currants to eggplant mixture. Season with vinegar, salt and pepper. Resume cooking for 5-10 minutes. Add more tomato juice if needed to keep caponata from becoming dry.

Serve warm on toasted baguette slices.

Turkey Cobb Sandwich

A sandwich makes a great lunch and with a bowl of soup – a great means of entertaining a crowd.

Serves 6

6 tablespoons mayonnaise
2 tablespoons Dijon mustard
12 slices bacon, about 250 g
6 generous bread rolls
500 g cooked turkey breast, sliced paper thin
6 slices tomato
2 avocados, peeled and sliced
2 cups finely shredded romaine or iceberg
    lettuce
6 tablespoons blue cheese dressing or
    6 tablespoons crumbled blue cheese

Combine the mayonnaise and mustard in a small bowl and set it aside. Grill or pan-fry the bacon until crisp, and set this aside, too.

Split the rolls and toast them under the grill. Spread the mustard-mayonnaise on the bottom half of each roll, then assemble the sandwiches in this order: 2 slices of bacon, a full layer of turkey slices, a slice of tomato, 3 or 4 slices of avocado, and lettuce. Spread blue cheese dressing on the top halves of the buns or crumble or a little blue cheese over the lettuce and close up the sandwiches. Cut the sand-wiches at an angle, if desired. Serve with plenty of napkins.

Turkey Cobb Sandwich

Salad Niçoise

Salad Niçoise evokes glorious memories of Nice – languid lunches on the French Riviera where the salads taste glorious and the scenery is equally so. If you venture to that part of the world, try the superb honey produced in Menton, near Nice. Both the salad and the honey just need a super-fresh baguette!

For a traditional Salad Niçoise you need new potatoes, green beans, tuna, red onion, capers, tomatoes, olives and hard-boiled eggs.

For our salad we unusually combined salad greens with favourite Niçoise-inspired ingredients. The real key to this salad is to use the freshest of ingredients.

Serves 2

2 cups salad greens
4 diced tomatoes
a handful of olives
2 spring onions, finely chopped
6-8 drained capers
6 lightly cooked green beans, cut in half
½ cup of your favourite herb-garlic vinaigrette
2 hard-boiled eggs, cut in half
olive oil
10 baby octopus

In a favourite salad bowl toss the salad greens, diced tomatoes, olives, spring onions, capers and beans. Dress with one half of the dressing, about ¼ cup.

Clean the baby octopus, making a small slit in the head and removing any membranes.

Heat a fry pan, with enough olive oil to cover the bottom of the pan and, when smoking, sear the baby octopus for 1 minute.

Then place the warm octopus on the salad with the hard-boiled eggs. Dribble the remaining dressing onto the salad and serve straight away.

Spinach and Salmon Roulade

250 g frozen spinach
60 g butter
⅓ cup flour
1 cup milk
4 large egg whites

Place spinach in pan and cook over moderate heat until all liquid has evaporated. Melt butter in separate pan, add flour and stir one minute.

Add milk gradually; stir until mixture boils and thickens.

Quickly stir in spinach and transfer mixture to a large bowl. Beat egg whites until soft peaks form. Fold lightly into spinach mixture.

Pour mixture into greased and grease-proofed, paper-lined Swiss roll (base measures 25 cm x 30 cm). Bake in hot oven 12 to 15 minutes or until puffed and golden brown. Remove from oven, turn onto wire rack covered with tea towel. Carefully remove lining paper, spread evenly first with mushroom mixture and then with salmon filling. Holding tea towel with both hands, gently roll roulade. Serve with a fresh homemade tomato sauce (see page 54).

SALMON FILLING: Combine 2 x 220 g cans red salmon (drained), 4 chopped shallots, ½ cup mayonnaise and 1 tablespoon chopped chives.

MUSHROOM MIXTURE: Chop and sauté 10 medium mushrooms in a little butter. Combine with 100 g softened cream cheese while still warm. Mix well.

....

NOTE: Years ago Wellington food writer and superb cook Catherine Wells made this roulade for lunch and served it with a luscious green salad.

Salad Niçoise

Scallops with Avocado-Corn Relish

This is a simply stunning combination. The crispness of the toasted pita breads, the crunchy corn, the creaminess of the avocado and the sweet, juicy scallops – yum!

Serves 4 as a starter

2 pita breads, halved and cut into quarters (16 pieces total)
olive oil
16 scallops, roe removed
6-8 tablespoons avocado-corn relish
3 tablespoons chives, finely chopped
2 tablespoons tomatoes, finely diced
additional fresh corn for garnish
Italian parsley for garnish

Place a little olive oil in a fry pan and cook the cut pita triangles for a few minutes on each side until golden on both sides. Keep warm.

Remove the oil from the pan. On a very high heat quickly sear the scallops for a few minutes. Take care not to overcook the scallops.

Place the avocado-corn relish on the warm pita triangles and top each portion with a scallop. Top the scallop with the diced tomato, additional corn and chives. Serve immediately.

Avocado-Corn Relish

Simply best described as a marriage made in heaven – try avocado with red onion, coriander, a little lime juice and a splash of jalapeño sauce.

1 avocado, coarsely chopped
½ cup freshly roasted or cooked corn kernels
2 tablespoons red onion, finely diced
¼ cup fresh coriander, finely chopped
a squeeze of lime juice
1 teaspoon jalapeño sauce,
1-2 tablespoons light sour cream
salt and freshly ground black pepper

Combine all the ingredients in a bowl and mix well. Season with salt and pepper. If you are making this ahead, place the avocado stone in the centre of the relish in the bowl and cover the top of the mixture with the avocado skins. This is a traditional Mexican solution to prevent avocados from browning. Cover and refrigerate.

Sir Anthony Hopkin's Favourite Salmon Pastrami

Sir Anthony Hopkins is often in residence at the Sheraton in Santa Monica, California. He frequently orders this for lunch and the chef kindly gave me the recipe.

Serves 4-6

1 kg side of fresh salmon, deboned
250 g salt
250 g brown sugar
1 teaspoon ground coriander
1 teaspoon ground allspice
1 teaspoon ground cloves
½ cup black cracked pepper
3 teaspoons crushed chilli flakes
2 large sliced oranges
4 small sliced lemons

Combine all the spices and rub on both sides of the salmon. Place in a stainless steel pan or ceramic dish. Layer the orange and lemon slices on top of the salmon, alternating each different fruit: lemon, orange, lemon, orange etc. Cover the entire pan with plastic wrap, or cover and place in fridge for 48 hours. Serve on grilled corn rye bread with cream cheese, shaved onions and fresh spinach.

Scallops with Avocado-Corn Relish

Thai Fish Salad

Ideal as a starter

Serves 4

1 mango or pawpaw
1 small red onion
1 red or yellow capsicum
1 telegraph cucumber
4 long mild chillies
pepper to taste
3-4 tablespoons fish sauce
4 teaspoons sugar
4 small tarakihi or snapper fillets
oil for grilling
handful of fresh coriander
25 g large roasted peanuts

Peel and dice the mango or pawpaw. Dice the red onion, capsicum and cucumber. Combine.

FOR THE DRESSING: Chop the chillies, discarding the seeds, then mix with pepper, fish sauce and sugar. Set aside.

Put the fish on an oiled foil-lined baking sheet and cook under a hot grill and cook 2-3 minutes each side.

Place the diced fruit and vegetable mixture on the plate. Place the fish on top. Drizzle the dressing over the fish. Garnish with coriander and scatter peanuts over the fish.

Warm Balsamic Vinaigrette for Fish

A great accompaniment to cooked fish. Add a few slow-roasted tomatoes to the plate for extra superb flavours.

3 crushed garlic cloves
100 ml olive oil
50 ml balsamic vinegar
salt and freshly ground black pepper
3-4 tablespoons chopped fresh herbs such as tarragon, basil, dill, chives or chervil.

Combine the crushed garlic cloves, olive oil and balsamic vinegar, salt and pepper. Place the mixture in a small saucepan and gently warm through. Toss in the fresh herbs. Spoon the vinaigrette over the fish and serve.

Nadeem's Chicken Curry

2 sliced onions
4 tablespoons curry powder
3 tablespoons tomato paste
2 tablespoons white vinegar
1 clove crushed garlic
1 small piece of crushed fresh ginger (1 tablespoon approximately)
1 kg chicken meat, diced
1 cup chicken stock
½ cup coconut milk
1 tablespoon coriander powder or 3 heaped tablespoons fresh coriander

Sauté the onions until golden brown, add the curry powder and stir. Then add the tomato paste, vinegar, garlic and ginger. Cook until it is dry, then add the chicken meat and cook covered on a slow heat.

Stir frequently. Add chicken stock.

When the chicken is cooked, add the coconut milk and simmer on a very low heat for 10 minutes.

Don't forget to add salt to taste as well as the coriander just before you serve. Serve with jasmine rice.

Pawpaw and Avocado Chicken Salad with Fresh Herb Dressing

Serves 6

6 cups cooked chicken meat

8 cups salad greens

1 fresh pawpaw, sliced

1 large red onion, finely sliced into rings

2 avocados, sliced

6 rashers bacon, rind removed and cut into strips

½ cup freshly toasted pine nuts

Roast your chicken according to the instructions given. Allow the bird to rest while the rest of the salad is quickly prepared.

Place the washed and prepared salad greens on a large platter. Slice or shred your chicken meat. If you choose to slice, make the pieces a manageable portion size. Scatter the chicken meat, pawpaw, onion rings, avocado and the freshly grilled bacon over the platter of salad greens in that order.

Drizzle with salad dressing and top with pine nuts.

....

NOTE: This salad is best served at room temperature. It's best served with slightly warm chicken and freshly grilled bacon.

Herb-parsley dressing:

½ cup oil

¼ cup white wine vinegar

1 teaspoon salt

2 teaspoons sugar

1 teaspoon freshly ground black pepper

1¼ teaspoons dry mustard

2 minced garlic cloves

⅓ cup finely minced parsley

3 tablespoons fresh basil or mint, chopped finely

Place all these ingredients in a jar with a secure and tight lid and shake well. Chill for several hours, or leave overnight so that the flavours blend together. Allow the dressing to come back to room temperature before re-shaking – then serve.

Fresh Tomato Sauce

1 chopped onion

olive oil

1 clove garlic, crushed

1 bay leaf

2 teaspoons parsley

2-3 teaspoons basil, fresh if possible – otherwise 1 teaspoon dried

6 whole tomatoes, chopped but not skinned

1 cup chicken stock

4 tablespoons tomato paste

pepper to taste

1 teaspoon sugar

Sauté onions in olive oil in a large saucepan. Add garlic, bay leaf, parsley, basil, tomatoes and chicken stock.

Simmer 1 hour with lid on. Add tomato paste and sugar. Season.

Strain through sieve to remove bay leaf and tomato skins. Serve warm (not hot) with roulade.

See page 48.

Afternoon Tea on the Sofa

There is nothing quite like the distinctive sound of
the kettle on the hob and the clink of tea cups to
draw you to the sofa for tea. Fill a tray with fine
tea cups, small silver spoons, fresh linen napkins,
slices of lemon, a bowl of sugar and a small jug of
milk. Pull out Aunt Agatha's cake stand and fill it
with luscious offerings. An afternoon tea like this
is a restorative experience!

Tuna and Chive Mini Quiche

These hot savouries are so popular they never have a chance to cool!

Makes about 24 mini quiches (5 cm in diameter)

Pastry:
120 g butter
120 g cream cheese
1 cup flour

Cream the butter and cream cheese. Add the flour and blend with a fork. Refrigerate for about 1 hour. Roll out to fit greased mini-quiche tins.

Filling:
125 g drained tuna
¼ cup spring onions, chopped
1 clove garlic, minced (optional)
2 large eggs
½ cup cottage cheese with chives
¼ cup milk
salt and pepper to taste
¼ cup grated cheese

Combine the tuna, spring onions and garlic, and divide the mixture between the pastry cases. Beat the eggs until frothy. Combine the cottage cheese, milk and seasonings. Fold into the eggs. Place approximately one tablespoon of the egg mixture over the tuna. Top the filling with grated cheese.

Bake at 190°C for 15-20 minutes until golden. Serve warm.

Roscoe's Lemon Butter Biscuits

By sprinkling the lemon juice over these biscuits before baking, you greatly enhance the fresh lemon flavour.

Makes about 32

175 g butter
½ cup sugar
2 teaspoons finely grated lemon rind
1¼ cups flour
pinch salt
additional sugar for rolling
juice from ½ lemon

Cream butter and sugar until the mixture is light and fluffy. Beat in lemon rind. Sift in flour and salt and mix together to form dough. Divide the dough in half and shape each portion into a sausage shape.

Wrap in plastic wrap and rest in fridge for at least 1 hour.

Unwrap and roll in additional sugar. Thinly slice the biscuit and arrange the slices on baking sheets. Sprinkle the tops with the lemon juice.

Bake at 180°C for 15-20 minutes or until golden brown. Cool on a wire rack.

Tuna and Chive Mini Quiche

The Classic Sandwich

Freshly made, delicate sandwiches are a perfect addition to an afternoon tea. When you make sandwiches and are not serving them straight away, store them in the refrigerator wrapped in a slightly damp tea towel to prevent them drying out.

Here are some suggested fillings:

- Curried chicken with walnuts on white bread
- Shrimp with dill vinaigrette on oatmeal bread
- Blue cheese crumbled over pears on oatmeal bread
- Cucumber with fresh mint on white bread
- Gentlemen's Relish on wholemeal bread
- Asparagus spears with a little lemon mayonnaise on wholemeal bread
- Cream cheese with walnuts and dates on raisin bread
- Savoury egg and lettuce on wholemeal bread with a herb mayonnaise
- Avocado with sprouts and a touch of fresh lemon on wholemeal bread
- Chicken and tarragon dressing on fresh white bread

Smoked Salmon Sandwich Spread

This is a very user-friendly, delicious sandwich spread.

100 g leftover smoked salmon (add more if it is available) or 213 g can salmon, drained
2 teaspoons chopped fresh dill
125 g spreadable cream cheese or softened regular cream cheese
2 tablespoons cream
salt and pepper to taste
juice of ½ lemon

Purée the salmon, chopped dill, cream cheese and just enough cream to smooth the texture. Taste the mixture at this point before adding the other ingredients.

You can add extra dill, but you do want the salmon flavour to dominate this spread. Store in the fridge.

Sydney Special Slice

A family favourite afternoon tea slice.

1 cup flour
½ cup sugar
1 cup corn flakes
1 level teaspoon baking powder
½ cup chopped walnuts and peanuts (combined)
140 g butter

Mix all the dry ingredients. Melt the butter, pour into the dry ingredients and mix well. Press into a buttered 30 cm x 25 cm flat tin. Cook for 30 minutes in a 160°C oven. Ice with a lemon icing while still warm. Cut into squares.

Serve on a jaunt with lashings of tea. Travels well in a tin.

Salmon and Egg
Club Sandwich

Sour Cream Lemon Cake

My good friend and fellow food writer, Robyn Martin, gave me this recipe years ago when I was in search of the ultimate lemon cake. It's a gem – try it!

250 g softened butter

2 cups sugar

6 lightly beaten large eggs

4 teaspoons finely grated lemon rind

2 cups flour

2 teaspoons baking powder

1 cup light sour cream

Glaze:
Juice of 1 lemon and ¼ cup sugar

Cream the butter and sugar until light and fluffy. Add the eggs and lemon rind, blend well.

Fold in flour and baking powder alternately with the sour cream. Mix gently until smooth and pour into a well greased 20 cm spring-bottom round tin. Bake 160°C for 60 minutes or until a skewer comes clean when tested.

After baking leave this cake in the tin for a few minutes, pour on the glaze. Leave for an additional few minutes and then remove from the pan.

....

NOTE: Serve with whipped cream and lemon curd.

Lemon Curd

125 g butter

250 g sugar

2 lemons

2 large eggs

Melt the butter gently into the sugar in a double saucepan.

Grate the zest of the lemon, avoiding all pith. Slowly add zest and lemon juice to the butter mixture.

Beat the eggs and gradually add them, stirring all the time to incorporate all the ingredients.

Cook gently until the mixture thickens smoothly. Don't be tempted to turn up the heat, if this thickening doesn't occur quickly. Gentle stirring and patience is the secret.

Irish Whiskey Cake

Make this cake when you want to sell your house, your car, your family or your dog. The aroma of this cake baking in the oven is so divine that any visitors will fall victim to your charms.

The peel of 1 large lemon

Irish whiskey

175 g butter

175 g sugar

175 g flour

3 large egg yolks

175 g sultanas

3 large egg whites

pinch of salt

1 teaspoon baking powder

Put the lemon peel into a glass and cover with a double measure (about 75 ml) of whiskey and leave overnight, covered. Cream the butter and the sugar until light. Add the yolks one at a time with a spoonful of sifted flour, mixing well. Strain the whiskey into it and add the sultanas with 2 tablespoons flour.

Whisk the egg whites until stiff and fold into the mixture with the remaining flour mixed with salt and baking powder. Make sure the mixture is well-mixed together.

Pour into a greased and lined 17.5 cm cake tin and bake at 180°C for 1¼-1½ hours. Check after approximately 65 minutes – if the skewer comes clean, it is ready. In a ring tin this mixture cooks in 55-60 minutes.

Cool for 5-10 minutes, then remove from the tin and remove the paper.

Sour Cream Lemon Cake with Lemon Curd

Christmas Cake

Every year I make this cake for friends and the requests for the recipe are so frequent I keep photocopies on hand. It's the best present to give anyone – no matter what the celebration. Try a piece with a good cheese, a good friend and a glass of port.

1 kg sultanas, chopped raisins
  and currants
250 g chopped apricots
250 g butter
1 cup brown sugar
½ cup brandy or orange juice
½ cup cold tea or water
3 teaspoons finely grated orange rind
2 teaspoons finely grated lemon rind
1 tablespoon treacle
5 large eggs lightly beaten
2 cups high-grade flour
1 teaspoon baking powder
½ teaspoon baking soda
whole blanched almonds
extra brandy

Line a deep 23 cm round or 20 cm square cake tin with three layers of paper, bringing paper 5 cm above the edge of the pan.

Combine sultanas, raisins and currants. Add apricots, butter, sugar, brandy/orange juice and cold tea in a large pot.

Stir over heat until butter is melted and sugar dissolved. Simmer, covered, 10 minutes; cool to room temperature.

Stir in orange and lemon rind. Add treacle and eggs. Then sift and add dry ingredients. Mix in with gentle, folding movements.

Spread mixture evenly into the prepared pan, decorate the top with almonds.

Bake in a slow 150°C oven for 2½ -3 hours. When the cake comes out of the oven, splash a little extra brandy over the top of the cake.

Cover hot cake with a tea towel, cool in pan.

NOTE: Glacé fruit and mixed peel do not appear in this recipe – I never include it in my Christmas baking.

If you want to include it in this recipe – do so – just subtract the other fruit quantities.

Date and Coconut Cake

A classic cake – date and coconut are happy partners.

1 cup chopped dates
1 cup boiling water
125 g butter
1 cup sugar
1 teaspoon vanilla
1 large egg
½ cup chopped walnuts
1½ cups flour
¼ teaspoon salt
1 teaspoon baking soda

Cover dates with hot water, leave until lukewarm. Cream butter and sugar, add vanilla and egg.

Beat well, add dates and liquid and remainder of ingredients.

Turn into a greased and floured 20 cm cake tin and bake at 180°C until almost cooked (about 45 minutes).

Spread the topping over the cake and bake it a further 10 minutes.

Topping:
4 tablespoons butter
½ cup brown sugar
2 tablespoons milk
1 cup coconut

Mix butter, sugar and milk in a saucepan. Bring to boil, remove from the heat and add coconut.

Salmon Pinwheel
(Recipe on page 68.)

Pine Nut Tart

Exercise great self control when buying pine nuts. Those small ivory-coloured nuts often seen in bulk bins in the supermarket need to be lightly handled; a heavy scoop can send the budget through the roof. This tart is a delicious sweet treatment of these popular nuts.

Serves 8-10

Pastry:
60 g soft butter
5 tablespoons caster sugar
¾ cup flour
2 large egg yolks
pinch salt

Filling:
125 g butter
½ cup caster sugar
2 large eggs
2 tablespoons sifted flour
125 g ground almonds
90 g pine nuts
3-4 tablespoons clear honey, warmed

PASTRY: Blend butter and sugar together, but do not cream. Add half the flour, work flour through with fingers. Add egg yolks, remaining flour and salt. Work to a dough. Chill for 30 minutes. Roll dough out on a lightly floured surface and place in a 24 cm fluted flan ring. Chill for 15 minutes. Preheat oven to 180 °C.

FILLING: Cream butter and sugar until light and fluffy. Add eggs one at a time. Add combined flour and ground almonds. Do not over mix. Place filling in pastry case. Smooth surface. Sprinkle with pine nuts. Bake for 25-30 minutes or until golden. Remove from oven, brush with warmed honey, bake for a further 5 minutes. Cool in ring before serving.

Bettie's Apple Cake

When I was 17 and living in Dover, Delaware (USA) my American mother Bettie Mestro would make a cake each Sunday. The sight of apples, cinnamon and sugar on the bench brought great joy to the family.

3 cups flour
1½ cups sugar
2 teaspoons baking powder
¼ teaspoon salt
4 large eggs, lightly beaten
250 ml vegetable oil
¼ cup orange juice
2½ teaspoons vanilla essence
2-3 apples, peeled and thinly sliced,
    eg: Granny Smith
1 teaspooon cinnamon and ¼ cup sugar
    mixed together

Place all the dry ingredients in a large bowl, add eggs, oil, orange juice and vanilla essence and mix together (this batter will be quite thick). Pour half the mixture into a greased 23-cm round baking tin. Cover with half the apples and half the cinnamon and sugar mixture. Repeat with batter. Finally arrange remaining apples over the batter and sprinkle with remaining cinnamon and sugar. Bake at 180°C for 1¼-1½ hours or until a skewer comes clean when tested. (This cake does take a long time to cook).

Delicious served warm by itself or when cool, cut into wedges and serve with cream.

Bettie's Apple Cake

Chocolate Cherry Slice

Former *Fair Go* presenter, Judith Fyfe, was busy making a slice one glorious Wellington afternoon when I called in for a cup of tea. Even before I sampled it, I knew it would be good. This warm enthusiast would always bake food with great flavour and appeal.

300 g dark chocolate
1 large egg
250 g glacé cherries, halved
½ cup caster sugar
150 g thread coconut

Line a Swiss roll tin with foil. Melt chocolate and spread on the base of the tin.

Beat the egg and add the remaining ingredients and spread over the chocolate.

Bake at 180°C for 15 to 20 minutes. Cool, then chill before slicing.

Cheese and Ham Pin Wheels

Hot savouries are super-popular for afternoon tea.

4 sheets puffed pastry*
1 large beaten egg
Salt and pepper to taste
200 g diced ham
1 large spring onion chopped (use the whole spring onion)
1½ cups grated cheese

Place the 4 pastry sheets on bench. Brush lightly with beaten egg, season with salt and pepper. Scatter the ham, spring onion and 1 cup of the grated cheese over the pastry sheets. Take care to leave 2 mm free of topping on each side. Roll up like a Swiss roll and press to seal. Trim the edges. Cut each sheet into 6 pieces approximately 4 mm. Press flat and place on greased tray. Brush with egg and scatter remaining ½ cup of cheese over pin wheels. Rest 15-20 minutes in the fridge, then bake at 220°C 15-20 minutes or until golden.

....

* 5 puffed pastry sheets (800 g) are available in the frozen food section of the supermarket.

** With our remaining puffed pastry sheet we made some extra special pin wheels using 100 g smoked salmon slices and 6 large spinach leaves that had been blanched quickly before use. We used the same egg wash, scattered ¼ teaspoon of poppyseeds over the pin wheels and baked in the same manner. (Photo on page 65.)

Apple Sauce Cake

The superb aroma and flavour of this cake always transports me back to my American mother's kitchen. I never thought a cake could bring back such warm, happy memories. It's moist and hugely popular.

425 g-500 g apple pulp
125 g butter, softened
1½ cups sugar
2 large eggs
2 cups flour
1½ teaspoon baking soda
½ teaspoon salt
½ teaspoon nutmeg
1 teaspoon cinnamon
½ teaspoon ground cloves
½ teaspoon allspice
1 cup raisins
½ cup chopped nuts

APPLE PULP: Either use a can of apple sauce or prepare your own apple sauce first. Apple pulp is easily prepared in the microwave. Place your sliced and peeled apples in a Pyrex glass container with no water or sugar. Cover and cook on high for 4-5 minutes. Mash with a potato masher and add sugar to taste. For this recipe go lightly on the sugar.

CAKE: Cream softened butter with sugar, add eggs and apple pulp. Then add all the sifted dry ingredients and gently fold in the raisins and nuts.

Place in a greased ring tin and bake at 180°C for 50-60 minutes or until a knife comes out cleanly when testing the cake.

....

NOTE: You do not ice this cake, but you can sprinkle sugar over the top of the cake 20 minutes into the cooking for an extra effect or dust with icing sugar after the cake has cooled. Serve with whipped cream and garnish with very finely cut slivers of lemon rind.

Peach Praline Pie

This pie was first introduced to me when I was catering diplomatic parties in Washington DC. Even top military personnel would get excited about this pie. Why not a slice of pie for afternoon tea? Search out your best source of fresh peaches for this recipe.

1 x 23 cm unbaked sweet shortcrust pastry
    pie shell
4 cups sliced peaches
½ cup sugar
2 tablespoons quick-cooking tapioca
1 tablespoon lemon juice
½ cup sifted flour
¼ cup brown sugar
½ cup chopped pecans
50 g butter

Combine peaches, sugar, tapioca, lemon juice in large bowl. Let stand 15 minutes.

Combine flour, sugar, pecans in a small bowl. Cut in butter until crumbly. Sprinkle ⅓ of these crumbs into pie shell. Cover with peaches. Top with remaining crumbs. Bake at 230°C for 10 minutes. Reduce to 180°C and bake 20 minutes or until peaches are tender and topping is brown.

Apple Sauce Cake

Dinner at Eight

Dinner at eight encourages an easy association with the great tastes of a special dinner, easy conversation, good wine and laughter. Sitting around the table with good friends and family is the perfect way to end the day. From a warm and casual family dinner to something more formal, simple well-prepared food accompanied by discussion makes everyone feel valued and loved. Even if our schedules are impossible, we still need to make the time for pleasure-filled occasions like these.

Grated Potato Casserole

This grated potato casserole is super popular. Perfect to use with barbecue meats, with cold meat, grilled fish or just a cooked egg!

Serves 4-6

4 medium potatoes, peeled
½ green capsicum, seeded and diced
1 onion, finely chopped
1 cup milk
3 large eggs
1½ teaspoons salt
1 teaspoon freshly ground black pepper
1 cup grated cheese
2 tablespoons soft butter

Grate potatoes and place in a large bowl with capsicum and onion. Put milk, eggs, salt, pepper, cheese and butter in a food processor or blender. Process, then mix well with the vegetables in the large bowl.

Place in a greased casserole and bake for one hour at 180°C.

....

NOTE: Capsicum is optional. You can use chopped chives or parsley from your garden instead or as well!

Rack of Lamb with Roasted Capsicum Salad

If you have never tried the superb combination of lamb and anchovies, let this recipe tempt you. The powerful anchovy flavour is diminished when cooked with lamb, but adds an extra roundness of flavour that is ideal. Coupled with a glorious roasted-capsicum salad, you have the Mediterranean on a plate. If you prefer not to use anchovies, you can just combine the garlic and parsley.

Serves 4

Lamb:
olive oil
4 lamb racks, trimmed
4 anchovy fillets
2 large cloves garlic, peeled and sliced in half
2 tablespoons freshly chopped parsley

Preheat oven to 220°C and heat oil in a frypan until smoking. Seal the meat well on all sides, taking particular care around the bone area. Place the anchovy fillets, garlic and parsley in a small food processor and process until well combined. If you do not have a small food processor, you can blend all these ingredients on your wooden board with a sharp knife. Smear this paste over the lamb and roast in the 220°C oven for 20-25 minutes.

Roasted Capsicum Salad:
6 roasted capsicums
6 tablespoons olive oil
3 large cloves garlic, chopped
2 tablespoons capers
2 tablespoons balsamic vinegar
2 tablespoons currants

Cut the roasted capsicums into strips as wide as your thumb. Gently sweat the garlic in the oil, until soft, but without colour. Add the capers, vinegar and currants. Bring to the boil, then put to one side until the currants swell. Mix with the capsicums. Season lightly with salt and freshly ground pepper.

Rack of Lamb with Roasted Capsicum Salad

Gratin Grand-Mere

Preparing vegetables for this dish is a pleasurable activity. After you wash and dice, you simply toss in a few herbs, garlic, oil and seasoning and after an hour's baking, they are totally scrumptious!

Serves 4

8 gourmet potatoes (large and good quality)
4 chopped courgettes
2 capsicums
good quality olive oil
sea salt
black pepper
6-8 cloves garlic
sprigs of fresh rosemary and thyme

Wash but do not peel potatoes. Slice into 2.5 cm chunks and place in a greased casserole dish with chunks of courgette and thick slices of capsicums.

Sprinkle with olive oil and salt, and a generous grinding of pepper. Toss gently.

Add garlic, rosemary and thyme. Cover and bake for one hour.

....
NOTE: Great with fish, tomato salsa and an adventurous green salad!

Carrots with Cumin and Ginger

Serves 6

Who said carrots are boring? Just try this combination of great flavours!

500 g carrots
55 g butter
1 tablespoon brown sugar
½ tablespoon white wine vinegar
1 tablespoon cumin seeds
1 tablespoon fresh ginger, finely chopped
2 tablespoons chopped parsley
Salt and pepper to taste

Steam or boil carrots until tender. (If young leave whole, otherwise cut into julienne strips.)

Place butter with sugar and vinegar in a saucepan and stir until everything has melted and combined.

Add cumin seeds and ginger then toss with the carrots and parsley.

Season with salt and pepper and place in a serving dish.

Potato Gratin

Serves 4-6

This is a rich and luscious treatment of potatoes. If you prefer something lighter, then the sliced potatoes can be scattered with garlic, a few knobs of butter, and covered with 150 ml milk and cooked the same way. Add a grinding of black pepper and the cheese if desired.

900 g potatoes, peeled and sliced
salt and pepper
1-2 garlic cloves, skinned and crushed
pinch of nutmeg, freshly grated
150 ml cream
75 g gruyere cheese, grated

Cook the potatoes in boiling salted water for five minutes, then drain well. Turn into a greased oven-proof dish.

Stir the seasoning, garlic and nutmeg into the cream and pour over the potatoes.

Sprinkle with cheese, cover and cook at 180°C for 45 minutes until potatoes are tender.

Uncover the dish and brown under a hot grill.

Serve our Potato Gratin with your favourite lightly steamed green vegetable topped with a knob of butter

Clark's Cajun Spice Mix

This recipe comes from my great friend and passionate cook, Julie Clark. She is well known as being the creative energy behind Wellington's Clark's in the Library.

This is an ever-popular and versatile spice mix – for example, it complements both chicken and fish well. Just be sure you keep it in an air-tight container, so it stays fresh.

4 tablespoons oregano
4 tablespoons thyme
4 tablespoons brown sugar
2 tablespoons black pepper
2 tablespoons white pepper
1 tablespoon paprika
2 tablespoons salt
2 tablespoons garlic powder
2 tablespoons garlic flakes
2 tablespoons onion flakes

Place all these ingredients in your food processor and whizz till fine and powdery. Store in a glass screw-top jar. The glass works best as it does not absorb any flavours. This mix keeps well and can be used on fish, chicken, squid and red meat.

Always give the jar a good shake before you use it. It's so simple to use. All you have to do is gently toss your fish or meat in the seasoning and bake.

NOTE: Make extra and give some as a gift to a friend. Just be careful when you mix this – the vapour can be quite overpowering.

Beef Fillet with Herb Crust

Super elegant and super simple – just ensure you use the best possible quality of beef for this recipe.

4 x 180-200 g beef fillet steaks
sea salt and black pepper
olive oil
3 slices white toast bread
5-6 tablespoons finely chopped parsley
2 cloves garlic, minced
125 g melted butter
a favourite mustard

Trim the fat and membrane from each beef steak and season with sea salt and black pepper. In a smoking hot pan, add olive oil and sear the meat until it is sealed all over. Allow 2 minutes each side. Leave to rest while you prepare the crust.

Crust: In a food processor, make the fresh bread crumbs and process the fresh parsley. Combine the bread crumbs with parsley in a bowl, season with salt and pepper. Add the garlic and melted butter.

Smear each steak with your favourite mustard. Place the crust on each fillet piling on top. Place in a 220°C oven for 15-20 minutes. Rest the meat for 10 minutes before serving. While the meat is resting prepare the sauce below.

NOTE: We served our beef fillet steaks with a super-simple tomato and pesto relish.

To make this relish gently heat one cup of your favourite tomato relish and ½ cup of pesto. You may thin to the desired sauce consistency with a little beef stock, but if you prefer a relish consistency, this is not required. If you do not require so much relish, then just use ½ cup of relish to ¼ cup of pesto.

Roscoe's Beef, Bacon and Stout Stew

Roscoe is the best friend a crazy cook could have, – totally understanding when the jam catches, the cat runs away with the fish, the oven is on the blink and it's only 9.00 am. He is rewarded with his favourite stew for "support beyond the call of duty".

1.5 kg rump steak, cut into large chunks
350 g bacon, diced
1 cup bacon or beef stock
355 ml can of stout
400 g tomato purée
1 tablespoon dried thyme
1-2 tablespoons brown sugar
3-4 cloves garlic, minced
2-3 medium onions
butter or oil
2 sticks celery, chopped
250 g mushrooms, sliced
3 carrots, peeled and chopped
black pepper to season

Dumplings:
2 cups flour
2 teaspoons baking powder
½ teaspoon salt
50 g butter
1 large egg
¾ cup milk
4 tablespoons finely chopped parsley

In a heavy frypan, sauté the bacon pieces with the beef chunks. The bacon fat provides enough moisture to prevent the beef catching on bottom of frypan. The beef is to be coloured but not completely cooked. Place in a crockpot or large casserole. When you have finished cooking the beef and bacon, deglaze the pan with the bacon or beef stock, scraping up all the brown bits and whisking constantly. After a few minutes, pour this over the beef. Pour the stout, tomato purée, thyme and brown sugar over the meat.

Sauté the garlic and onions until soft and lightly browned. Do not allow to burn. If there is not sufficient bacon fat, just add a little butter or oil. Add cooked onions to the meat. Now gently cook the cut-up celery, mushrooms and carrots for a few minutes and add to the crockpot or casserole. Season. Cook on low heat in the crockpot for 10-12 hours or in a low, covered oven at 150°C for 2 hours. If you have used a crockpot you can transfer to a casserole, put dumplings on top and place in a preheated 180°C oven.

For the dumplings, sift the dry ingredients, work in the butter as for scones. Mix together egg and milk, add to the butter mixture. To this wet dough, add chopped parsley. Place in rough round shapes on top of the stew and bake for another 30 minutes at 180°C.

Chicken with Scallops and Bacon

In this recipe a chicken breast with the wing bone intact is used to give greater flavour. Bone-in meat always has superior flavour.

olive oil
4 chicken breasts, wing bone in
12-20 scallops
4 rashers bacon

Add olive oil to frypan until bottom is just covered. When smoking, add the chicken and sear until golden brown. Allow 2-3 minutes on one side and seal the other side for approximately 2 minutes. Place in a 200°C oven for 20-25 minutes.

10 minutes before the end of the chicken cooking time place the bacon on a baking tray in the oven. When the bacon and chicken have almost completed their cooking, place a light coating of olive oil in your frying pan, heat until smoking and quickly sear the scallops. Within a few seconds in a hot pan, the scallops will change colour and be ready – always try to keep the cooking time to a minimum to avoid a rubbery-textured scallop. Place the chicken breast on a warmed serving plate with a rasher of bacon and 3-5 scallops.

You can serve this chicken with either a tarragon beurre blanc (butter sauce) a simple tomato sauce or a fresh tomato salsa (see page 54).

Chicken with Scallops and Bacon

Lamb Shanks

This recipe is an adaptation of Alister Brown's sensational treatment of lamb shanks. True to this Wellington chef's philosophy that good food does not need to be tortured or over processed, this recipe creates divine flavours.

8 rashers bacon
2 cups onions, roughly chopped
1 cup carrots, roughly chopped
1 cup celery, roughly chopped
4 cloves garlic, roughly chopped
6 to 8 lamb shanks
1½ cups port
2 tablespoons tomato paste
2 cups beef stock
2 tablespoons fresh rosemary
3 bay leaves
2 tablespoons brown sugar
30 g butter
30 g flour
1.5 kg potatoes
salt and pepper to season

In a large saucepan, add bacon and brown over medium heat. Add chopped onions, carrots, celery and garlic. Increase heat to caramelise vegetables.

Meanwhile dust the lamb shanks in seasoned flour and brown in a hot sauté pan. Add shanks to the vegetables in the saucepan, then cover with the port, tomato paste and beef stock. Add the chopped rosemary, bay leaves and brown sugar. Bring to low boil, cook (covered) for about 2½ hours or until the meat is tender.

Remove the shanks with a slotted spoon. In a separate saucepan melt the butter, add the flour and mix. Spoon some of the broth into the roux and whisk to eliminate any lumps. Add the thickened sauce to the main stew base, add the chopped potatoes and simmer for 20 minutes. Season with salt and pepper. Remove from heat and place the shanks back in the stew. Serve piping hot. May be made three days ahead or frozen and used when desired.

NOTE: For our lamb shank dinner we served minted pea purée, kumara purée with slow-roasted garlic and onions. As we were roasting the garlic and onions, we also oven-roasted the shanks using this recipe. Brown the lamb shanks in hot oil, place in a 220°C oven for 10 minutes; then turn down to 200°C and cook for one hour uncovered. Just make sure you have the beef stock/port sauce to cover the shanks.

Minted Pea Purée

Serves 4-6

500 g potatoes, peeled
½ onion, peeled and roughly chopped
3 cups frozen green peas, thawed
2 tablespoons finely chopped mint
100 g butter
salt and pepper

Cut the potatoes into even pieces. Bring to the boil in salted water, add the onions and cook until the potatoes are soft.

Add the peas and bring back to the boil. Drain off the water. Place the mixture in a food processor, add the mint and butter. Blend until smooth. Check for salt and pepper. Return to a clean pot, add a knob of butter and gently heat.

NOTE: For a kumara purée, just cook 250 g peeled potatoes and 250 g peeled kumara with the ½ peeled and roughly chopped onion. When cooked, drain and add the 100 g butter, season with salt and pepper. To make it extra luscious, you could add a little cream to this mixture.

Lamb Shanks

Herb and Pepper Crusted Salmon with Corn

This superb treatment of salmon was created by top Wellington chef Chris Green of Boulcott Street Bistro. This recipe has become one of the most popular dishes on his menu. Chris manages to maintain a very relaxed, down-to-earth approach to food, but he never tires of pushing the boundaries to achieve great flavours and memorable dining.

Serves 4

4 x 200 g fillets of fresh salmon
1 cup olive oil
the juice of two lemons
1 crushed garlic clove
⅓ cup soy sauce
2 cups whole kernel sweetcorn
2 cups cream
¾ cup parsley, chopped
1 bunch chervil, chopped
¼ cup crushed peppercorns
additional olive oil
½ cup red capsicum, diced

Marinate the salmon fillets in olive oil, lemon juice, crushed garlic and soy sauce for 30 minutes.

Heat the corn and cream in a saucepan until boiling. Reduce the heat and simmer until the liquid has reduced to a sauce consistency. (Approximately 15-20 minutes).

Remove the salmon and pat dry. Place on a greased oven tray, skin side down. Liberally cover with chopped parsley, chervil and peppercorns. Drizzle with olive oil and cook under the grill for 7-10 minutes, until medium rare only.

Spoon creamed corn onto hot plates, sprinkle with red capsicum. Place salmon fillet on the corn. Garnish with half a lemon, more red capsicum, and cracked pepper.

Barbecued Salmon

fresh salmon fillet (approximately 1 kg)
½ cup honey
1 tablespoon soy sauce
2 tablespoons brandy
¼ cup white wine
1 tablespoon chopped fresh ginger
2-4 small chillies, depending on taste
3 crushed Kaffir lime leaves
15 chopped juniper berries
1 tablespoon chopped fresh coriander
¼ cup vinegar
1 tablespoon freshly chopped basil

Mix all the ingredients together. If using dried Kaffir lime leaves, you may wish to pre-soak them before using in the marinade. Remove the skin from the salmon and the bones. Use kitchen tweezers to remove the fine salmon bones.

Pour the marinade over the salmon and leave for about four hours. Cook the side of salmon on a hot barbecue for three minutes on each side: the fish should be medium rare.

The remains of the marinade can be served to pour over the cooked salmon.

....

NOTE: Serve with Potato Gratin (see page 76) and a big green salad.

Herb and Pepper Crusted Salmon with Corn

Pork Steaks and Shiitake Sauce

This recipe truly celebrates the delicious flavour of fresh shiitake mushrooms. We added pork steaks, fresh asparagus and risotto to make a sensational combination.

Pork Steaks:

8 pork loin steaks (about 750 g total weight, pounded)
black pepper
olive oil
1 egg
freshly grated Parmesan cheese to sprinkle

Coat a frypan with olive oil and heat until smoking. Season your pork steaks with black pepper and seal in the hot pan (one minute each side). Remove from the pan and allow to cool slightly. Beat the egg, dip the pork steaks in the egg and sprinkle with freshly grated Parmesan cheese.

Place in a hot oven 220°C for 10-12 minutes.

Shiitake Sauce

Use a variety of fresh mushrooms if fresh shiitake is not available. This sauce works superbly with pasta or as a topping for grilled polenta.

½ medium onion, finely chopped
1 teaspoon fresh ginger, finely minced
2 cloves garlic
2 tablespoons sesame oil
200 g shiitake mushrooms, sliced
1 tablespoon soy sauce
1 cup cream
pepper for seasoning
1 teaspoon arrowroot
1 teaspoon water
2-3 tablespoons freshly chopped coriander
50 g hard butter

Sauté the onion, ginger and garlic in the sesame oil for 2 minutes. Add the sliced mushrooms (making sure the stems are removed). When they are soft, cook for approximately another 2 minutes, then add the soy sauce. Let mixture simmer for a few more minutes and add the cream.

Mix the arrowroot and water together and add to the sauce, stirring well. Simmer and cook this slowly for a few more minutes. Add the coriander and check the seasoning just prior to serving.

Finish by adding the butter to provide extra gloss and flavour.

Pumpkin Pudding

When I was living in Washington DC, a neighbour very kindly offered to cook me Thanksgiving dinner, and this pumpkin pudding was a scrummy addition to the roast turkey. Try it and see for yourself. You will be delighted with this savoury treat.

Serves 4-6

2 slices of bread
¼ cup sugar
½ lemon, grated rind only
¾ cup orange juice
½ cup chopped peanuts
180 g butter
3 cups cooked pumpkin

Break slices of bread into small pieces and mix with sugar, lemon rind, orange juice, peanuts, butter, and pumpkin.

Place in a greased casserole dish. Bake 180°C oven for 30-45 minutes.

NOTE: You can dot the top of the casserole with extra cubes of bread and a little melted butter, if desired.

Thai Chicken Curry

The ever-popular Thai chicken curry! So easy to make, and the results are superb. Fresh chicken breasts or boneless chicken thighs (allow 2 per serving) are preferable to frozen chicken in this recipe.

Serves 4

2 whole chicken breasts, skin removed
1 tablespoon dark soy sauce
½ cup flour
2 tablespoons oil
1-2 teaspoons green curry paste
1-2 cloves garlic, finely minced
1 teaspoon finely chopped ginger
1 spring onion, chopped
400 ml coconut cream
2 tablespoons sugar
1-2 tablespoons fish sauce
1 tablespoon soy sauce
fresh coriander for garnish

Cut breasts into bite-sized pieces. Place in a bowl, add the soy sauce to chicken and stir.

Sprinkle the flour over the chicken and stir gently to coat the chicken.

Sauté chicken in the oil and remove from the pan when golden on both sides.

Add curry paste to pan and cook for 1-2 minutes, add garlic, ginger and onion – sauté for a few minutes. Return the chicken to the pan and add the coconut cream, sugar, fish sauce and soy sauce.

Lower heat and simmer for 15 minutes until chicken is cooked through.

Garnish with fresh chopped coriander.

....

NOTE: Serve with jasmine rice and cucumber raita.

Moroccan Seasoning for Fish Fillets

Serves 4

800 g gurnard fillets, skinned and boned
salt and pepper
⅓ cup onion, very finely diced
1 clove garlic, crushed
⅓ cup coriander, very finely chopped
⅓ cup parsley, very finely chopped
1 teaspoon cumin seeds
1 teaspoon paprika
juice of 1 lemon
½ cup olive oil
pinch of cayenne pepper
hot oil for cooking

Lightly dust the gurnard fillets with salt and pepper and place in a deep tray. Mix all the remaining ingredients together except for the hot oil for cooking. Pour this marinade over the fillets and marinate for at least one hour.

Remove from the marinade and cook for a few minutes on each side in hot oil until light brown. Turn and finish cooking. Serve with lemon wedges. Always cook your fresh fish medium-rare.

Moroccan Fish

Blueberry Buttermilk Tart

A slice of tart to finish a meal; simple, yet stylish.

sweet short pastry
1 cup buttermilk
3 large egg yolks
½ cup sugar
1 tablespoon freshly grated lemon zest
1 tablespoon fresh lemon juice
125 g butter, melted and cooled
1 teaspoon vanilla essence
pinch of salt
2 tablespoons flour
2 cups blueberries

Line a greased 25 cm pie plate with pastry. Prick the pastry and bake blind with foil and with beans or rice to weigh down the pastry for 25 minutes. Remove the foil and beans/rice and bake for another 5 to 10 minutes until it is a pale golden colour.

In a blender or food processor combine all the ingredients except the blueberries.

Place the berries in the tart base – pour the filling over the top. Bake 180°C for 30-35 minutes or until the filling is set. When cool dust with icing sugar.

....

NOTE: If you are using frozen berries – allow extra cooking time.

Vanilla Panna Cotta

Elegance on a plate – and delicious with poached stone fruits!

Serves 6

3 cups cream
1 cup milk
the seeds from 4 vanilla pods or 1 tablespoon vanilla essence
¾ cup sugar
4 sheets of gelatine

Slowly bring the cream, milk, vanilla and sugar to the boil. Soak the gelatine leaves in cold water for approx 10 minutes. Squeeze out the excess water from the gelatine leaves, stir into the cream. When dissolved, strain the mixture into a large jug. Allow mixture to cool completely. Pour into moulds. (We used 120 ml moulds.) Cover moulds with plastic wrap and refrigerate for 4 hours.

Serve with poached or roasted stone fruits.

....

NOTE: If sheets of gelatine are not available you can use 4 teaspoons of gelatine. To release the panna cotta from the mould, just dip the mould in warm water for a few seconds. Then with the back of a knife, carefully loosen the top of the panna cotta and turn out.

Supper in the Cook's Library

Supper conjures up cosy images: lying by the fire with a pile of good books, eating comfort food, rain on the roof, old sweaters and slippers. My library at home, with over a thousand cookbooks, always encourages anyone with even the smallest interest in food. I started collecting them when I was ten, so inspiration for supper dishes is not difficult!

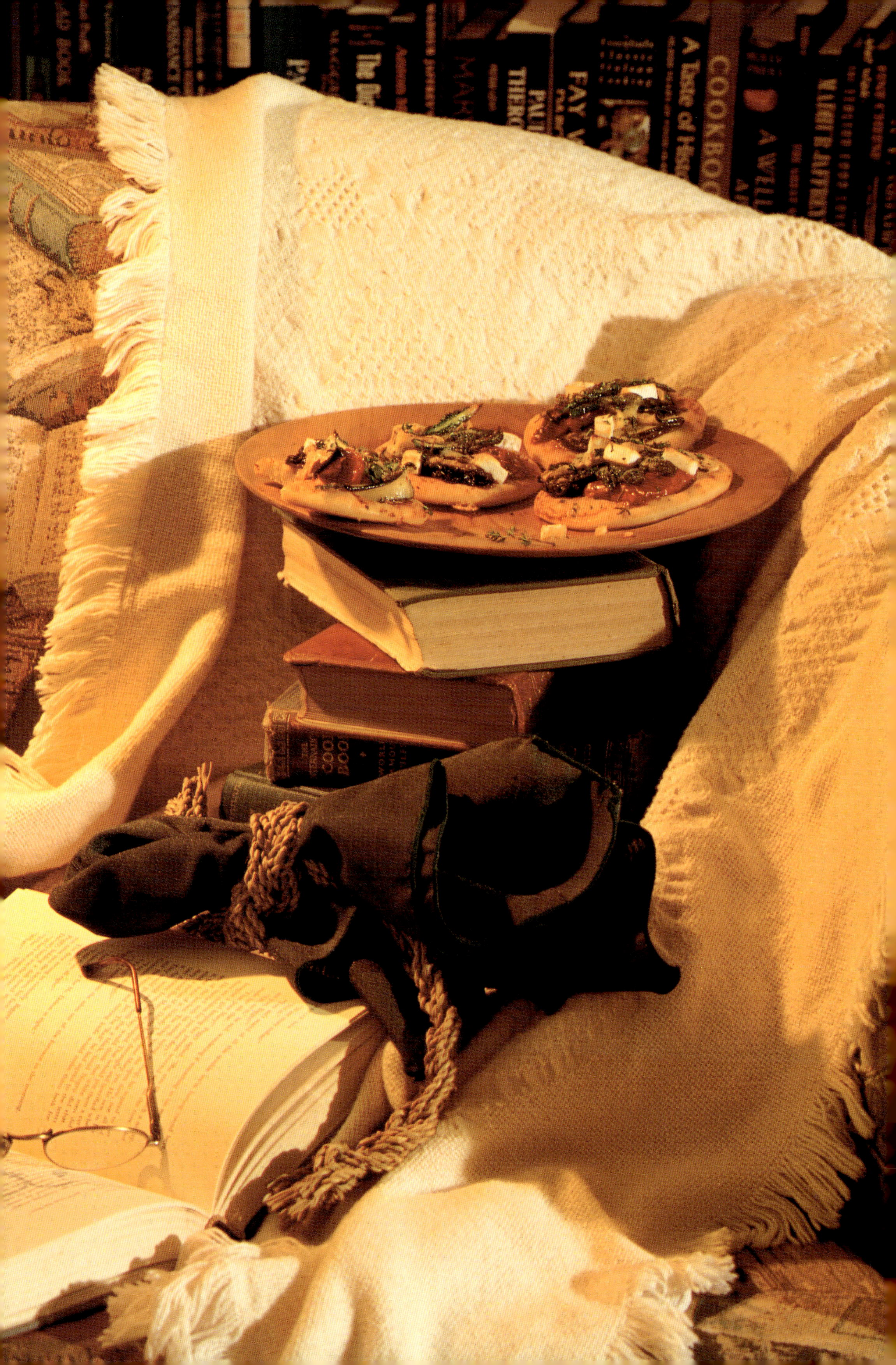

Mini Savoury Pizzas

Use a variety of toppings with your pizza bases. Making pizzas can be a fun, family activity – especially on a wet weekend.

(4 x 18 cm bases)
1 cup luke-warm water
½ cup milk, room temperature
1 tablespoon dried yeast
1 teaspoon sugar
500 g or 3½ cups flour
2 teaspoons olive oil
2 teaspoons salt
Toppings (a fresh, thick tomato purée, grilled vegetables, blanched asparagus, sun-dried tomatoes, fresh herbs, feta)

Mix the warm water, milk, yeast and sugar. Leave in a warm place for approximately 10 minutes. Mix with the flour, olive oil and salt. To form a dough, knead for 5-10 minutes until smooth and elastic .

Roll out, cut out circles, brush with tomato purée, and top with a variety of grilled vegetables, blanched asparagus, sun-dried tomatoes, fresh herbs and feta.

Bake at 220°C for 12-15 minutes.

Ruth's Swede Soufflé

Ruth, a friend of my mother's, gave me this recipe when I first started publishing recipes. She said that even if you don't like swedes, or if someone in your family does not like them, make the soufflé and don't tell them what's in it. They will never know how good it is for them or what exactly is in the recipe, but they'll surely want more.

50 g butter
2 tablespoons flour
½ cup milk
3 large eggs
500 g swede, mashed and seasoned with salt and pepper. (This is easier if cooked in the microwave. You can use more swede if you like).

Melt butter, add flour and milk. Let boil for 1-2 minutes. Cool slightly. Separate eggs. Beat yolks and stir into the sauce. Add swede. Beat egg whites and fold in. Cook in an ungreased dish at 190°C for 20-25 minutes.

In Scotland, swedes and potatoes are often served together and affectionately known as "Neeps and Tatties". Here is a tasty way to serve potatoes to complement this swede soufflé dish.

Tatties

Layer sliced potatoes, chopped onions and grated cheese in a greased dish. Cover and microwave or bake covered for ½ hour in a 160°C oven. This recipe does not require milk or a cream sauce. Microwave time depends on the amount of potatoes. Try cooking for a few minutes, check progress with a knife, and serve when potatoes are soft.

Honey Apple Crisp

A family favourite – the mixture of honey, apples and the hint of lemon makes this a great dessert.

4 cups tart apples, sliced
¼ cup sugar
2 tablespoons lemon juice
½ cup honey
½ cup flour
¼ cup brown sugar
¼ teaspoon salt
¼ teaspoon cinnamon
70 g butter
a couple of extra knobs of butter

Spread the apple slices in a casserole and sprinkle with sugar, lemon juice and honey. Mix the flour, brown sugar, salt and cinnamon and cut in the butter until the mixture resembles coarse cornmeal.

Spread the topping evenly over the apples and dot with a few extra knobs of butter. Bake at 190°C for 30-40 minutes or until the apples are tender and the crust crisp and brown.

Serve with custard, cream or ice cream, or why not all three?

Raisin Pudding

Again, the addition of lemon brings out an extra dimension to this pudding, and makes it perfect comfort food.

1 cup self-raising flour
pinch of salt
¼ cup sugar
45 g butter
1 cup raisins
1 lemon rind, finely grated
½ cup milk

Sift flour and salt together with sugar. Lightly rub in butter with raisins and lemon rind. Add milk. Mix to form a soft dough. Spread out evenly in a greased 20 cm x 20 cm ovenproof dish.

Sauce:
2 cups boiling water
1 cup brown sugar
65 g butter

Put boiling water, sugar and butter in saucepan and heat until butter melts. Spoon over contents of dish. Bake at 180°C for approximately 45-60 minutes. Serve while hot with cream or custard or both.

Raisin Pudding

Lamb and Olive Balls

You often associate beef with meat balls, but these delicious meat balls bring a taste of the Mediterranean with lamb, feta and olives combined. The coriander gives them extra freshness.

Serves 4

3 slices white or whole wheat bread
1 kg fairly lean ground lamb
125 g feta, crumbled
1 cup Kalamata olives, pitted and chopped
1 large egg, beaten
½ tablespoon cinnamon
½ teaspoon hot dried chilli flakes
3 garlic cloves, crushed
1 bunch coriander, chopped
3 tablespoons olive oil

Cut the crusts from the bread; soak the slices in water, wring them out, and crumble them. With your fingers, mix the lamb well with the bread, feta, olives, egg, cinnamon, chilli flakes, garlic, and coriander. Form into 20 small meatballs.

In a heavy frying pan, cook the meatballs in the olive oil until crisp and brown on one side; then turn and brown the balls on all sides, no more than 10 minutes, over a fairly high heat. The meat should be medium rare.

....

TIP: To pit Kalamata olives, which are soft, just press down on them with your thumb and the pits will come right out, or use a pitter.

NOTE: For this cookbook we made large meat balls to accompany our pasta, which was flecked with fresh herbs from the garden. Allow extra cooking time for the larger meat balls.

Chicken Pie with Scone Crust

Designed for a fireside supper, this pie has all the flavours of your grandmother's kitchen.

Serves 4

Filling:
4 cups chicken stock
3 carrots, cut into chunks
400 g potatoes, peeled and cut into chunks
3 ribs celery, cut into chunks
4 cups cooked, cubed chicken meat
1 large onion
6 tablespoons butter
6 tablespoons flour
½ teaspoon thyme
¼ teaspoon ground nutmeg
½ cup chopped parsley

In a saucepan bring chicken stock, carrots, potatoes and celery to a boil. Simmer vegetables uncovered for 10 to 15 minutes, or until tender. Transfer vegetables to a large bowl. Add chicken meat. Put the chicken stock to one side.

In another saucepan cook onion in butter over low heat, until soft. Add flour and cook the roux for 3 minutes. Add reserved chicken stock. Whisk well.

Bring mixture to the boil and add thyme. Stir for 5 minutes. Stir in nutmeg and chopped parsley. Add to chicken mixture and place in a greased casserole dish.

SCONE CRUST: Make your favourite cheese scone recipe, add some chopped chives or parsley and use buttermilk or milk and one egg as the liquid. Form a dough, cut out your shapes, place on top of the chicken. Brush with eggwash. Bake at 210°C for 15-25 minutes or until the scones are puffed and golden and the filling is bubbling.

Lamb and Olive Balls

Lai's Self-saucing Chocolate Pudding

My delightful sister-in-law, Lai, is a wonderful cook and her puddings are legendary. This pudding is so simple, but everyone wants more!

Serves 4

50 g butter
½ cup milk
1 teaspoon vanilla essence
1 cup flour
1 teaspoon baking powder
1 tablespoon cocoa
½ cup sugar

Sauce:
½ cup brown sugar
1 tablespoon cocoa
1-½ cups hot water

Heat the butter, milk and vanilla until the butter melts. Sift the flour, baking powder and cocoa and mix with the sugar.

Pour the warm milk mixture onto the flour mixture and mix until smooth.

Place in a 20 cm x 20 cm greased baking dish.

SAUCE: Mix the brown sugar with the cocoa and sprinkle on top. Pour on the hot water, do not stir.

Bake at 180°C for approximately 35 minutes. Serve with custard.

Jazz Bar Brownies

We staggered into the *Jazz Bar Café* in Queenstown after walking the Milford Track. Their chocolate brownies tasted so good we asked for the recipe. These are scrummy!

2½ cups chocolate chips
350 g butter
1 tablespoon vanilla essence
2 tablespoons instant coffee
5 large eggs
2 cups sugar
2½ cups flour
2 cups chopped cashew nuts
Icing sugar

Melt chocolate chips, butter, vanilla essence and instant coffee in the top of a double boiler, stirring occassionally until the mixture is smooth. Whisk eggs and sugar well until the mixture is thick and creamy. Beat into the cooled chocolate butter mixture. Fold in flour and cashew nuts. Pour into a greased, deep 25 cm x 30 cm tin and bake at 180°C for approximately 30-35 minutes or until firm around edges but still soft in centre. Cool, then cut into squares. Dust with icing sugar.

Lai's Self-saucing Chocolate Pudding

Seafood Fritters

People get excited when you mention the word 'fritter'. The associations can be so pleasant – memories of sweet corn fritters with bacon for Sunday family tea, pipi fritters after a day at the beach with your family, the classic West Coast whitebait fritter; even the delicious results when the cook has cleaned out the fridge and made stunning fritters with left-over vegetables and cold roast meat.

When they are well prepared fritters are a memorable combination of crunch and flavour. Serve with fresh and tangy salsa or dipping sauce and the results are scrumptious.

Stunning fritter combinations include;

- seafood or chicken with vegetable and coriander
- sweet corn with sweet chilli sauce (add a few peas for extra colour)
- smoked fish and spring onions
- wild rice and duck
- hot deep-fried par-cooked fennel segments to serve with a loin of pork
- salmon and dill
- eggplant served with sweet pepper sauce and creme fràiche
- potato and bacon
- lemon and sheep's milk cheese with honey for dessert
- pork and apple

Food is less greasy when fried in lots of oil rather than in small amounts, and if the oil in the pan is the right temperature, the food absorbs less oil. For example, heat oil until not quite smoking, and add a teaspoon of mixture to the pan and if it browns quickly you are ready to go.

Crisp the fritter on one side (you want a nice golden colour before you turn it over) and then turn down the heat to cook the other side. This way the fritter cooks evenly through without burning.

When using raw seafood and chicken, just cook lightly before you add to the batter. It's not necessary to pre-cook oysters or whitebait but steam mussels first and lightly sauté or poach the raw chicken.

These mussel and courgette fritters were served with a homemade tartare sauce and as I was preparing a scallop dish at the same time, I had the scallop roe to use up, but any other seafood could have been lightly cooked and used.

Mussel and Courgette Fritters

12 mussels
12 scallop roe, optional
¾ cup flour
salt and freshly ground black pepper to taste
3 large eggs
½ cup milk
¼ cup parsley, roughly chopped
1 spring onion, finely chopped
2 courgettes, grated
2 cloves garlic, finely minced

Steam open the mussels and lightly cook the scallop roe in a hot pan. Put flour, salt and pepper in bowl. Mix eggs and milk together with a whisk in a separate bowl. Start slowly and pour the egg and milk mixture into the flour to make a paste, then, as you add more liquid, it will become a smooth batter. Continue to beat until well blended and with a smooth consistency. Add all the remaining ingredients. Cook in oil and have the pan medium-hot as described above.

NOTE: Serve with homemade tartare sauce or tomato salsa. With our fritters we served oven fries. A fun version of fish and chips!

Mussel Chowder

If you have a good friend who is very busy and often cooks for one, make up a batch of this delicious chowder and give it to them as a present. It's a great meal in a bowl. In my kitchen I have some special large glass clip-top jars which I fill with chowder on the understanding that when the empty jar is returned, a refill will be made. It is amazing how quickly these jars arrive back on the kitchen bench.

Serves 4

25 mussels (remove beards and scrub shells)
15 g butter
3 bacon rashers, finely chopped
1 red capsicum, finely chopped
1 small onion, finely chopped
2 tablespoons flour
1½ cups milk
1 cup fish stock
2 small potatoes, finely chopped
2 spring onions, finely chopped
4 tablespoons parsley, freshly chopped

Add mussels to a large saucepan of boiling water, reduce heat, cover, and simmer for about 2 minutes or until shells have opened. Remove mussel meat from shells.

Heat butter in another saucepan and add bacon, red capsicum and onion. Cook over medium heat for 5 minutes.

Add flour and stir for 1 minute. Remove from heat and gradually stir in milk and fish stock. Add potatoes and stir over high heat until mixture boils and thickens.

Reduce heat, add chopped mussels, spring onions and parsley. Reheat mixture without boiling.

....

NOTE: You can add corn, peas and mixed vegetables to this chowder if you desire.

Ma's Pea and Ham Soup

My mother's pea and ham soup should be prescribed to all of us who need an extra lift during the winter months. Even after a terrible day when your car has blown up and you have had a hellish day at the office, a bowl of this soup will help you think it's a day in paradise. Like eating a great Greek salad, consuming a good pea and ham soup makes you feel stronger and perhaps a little heroic!

2 cups green split peas
8 cups water
1 bacon hock or ham bone or a handful of
   bacon rinds
2 bay leaves
4 carrots
1 medium onion, chopped
freshly ground black pepper
salt to taste and chopped parsley

Place the peas, water, bacon hock and bay leaves in a large stock pot and cook gently for 2-3 hours.

Keep an eye on the soup as it thickens. You will need to add more water as it gently cooks.

Peel and chop carrots and place with chopped onion in a food processor. Use the metal blade, and the mixture will quickly become a fine dice. Place this in the soup pot with black pepper to taste. Cook for another hour. Just before serving, remove bacon hock, pull the meat away from the bone and place half the meat back into the soup. The remaining meat is great for sandwiches and bread rolls.

Remove the bay leaves and add parsley and salt to taste.

Do not add the salt before this stage. If salt is added any earlier, the split peas will not cook down.

Ma's Apple Sponge

This is a simple recipe which produces outstanding results on any hot, stewed fruit. However, to ensure superb results, make sure your sponge mixture is placed on top of hot fruit. In other words, make the sponge while the fruit is gently simmering.

It works well on hot apples, apricots, rhubarb, nectarines or pears. Use enough fruit to fill your favourite medium casserole ½ to ⅔ full of peeled, sliced fruit.

Stewed fruit:

2 large eggs at room temperature

¾ cup sugar

1 cup sifted flour

1 teaspoon baking powder

1 tablespoon melted butter

1-2 tablespoons milk

1 teaspoon vanilla

Stew your fruit, adding a small amount of sugar for flavour at the end of the cooking process. By adding it at the end, you always use less sugar.

While the fruit is cooking, beat the eggs with the sugar. Beat together until pale, thick and foamy (approximately 2-3 minutes).

Add sifted flour and baking powder. Fold flour mixture gently into egg mixture with fork.

Melt butter in milk and add to the mix. Finally, add vanilla.

Pour over piping hot fruit in oven-proof dish.

Bake at 180°C for approximately 30 minutes or until done. Test with a skewer.

Serve warm. Lightly dust the sponge with sifted icing sugar and serve warm with cream or custard.

Ma's Stuffing for Chicken

This stuffing makes enough to fill the cavity of a size 9 bird.

30 g butter

½ onion, finely chopped

2 cups fresh bread crumbs

1 diced apple, peeled

2 rashers bacon (optional)

½ cup chopped fresh herbs (parsley, sage, thyme, dill, rosemary, chives, oregano)*

salt and freshly ground black pepper to taste

½ cup sultanas or other dried fruits like chopped apricots or chopped prunes

Place the chopped onion in a bowl with the butter and microwave on high for 3-4 minutes. Add the rest of the ingredients and mix well. If you like, add bacon to the stuffing – cook first and add.

Remember with poultry – it is important to always have the stuffing and the bird at the same temperature. Placing a hot stuffing in a very cold bird is not advised. Let the stuffing cool slightly before placing inside the bird.

....

NOTE: This may seem like a heavy measure of fresh herbs and you can certainly reduce the quantity if you prefer, but my pleasure in visiting the vegetable garden to cut fresh herbs for the stuffing is a highlight in the preparation, and our family just loves the intensity of mixed herb flavour you get with this recipe.

Wrap your stuffed chicken with bacon and bake as you would normally – allowing extra time for a stuffed chicken.

Blueberry and Apricot Upside-down Cake

Topping:

60 g butter

¾ cup brown sugar

1 400 g can apricots, drained

1 punnet blueberries

Melt butter on low heat and sprinkle brown sugar – leave for a few minutes on low. Remove from heat. Pour into your cake tin and arrange fruits.

Batter:

2 cups flour

1 teaspoon baking powder

1 teaspoon baking soda

pinch of salt

125 g cup soft butter

1 cup sugar

2 teaspoons vanilla essence

2 large eggs

1 cup buttermilk

Sift flour, baking powder, baking soda, salt. Cream butter and sugar. Add vanilla essence, then eggs one at a time. Beat well. Add buttermilk, then stir in dry ingredients. Spoon over fruit evenly (be careful not to move fruit). Cook in the middle of the oven at 350°C for 40-45 minutes or until top springs back.

Run knife around side immediately – turn over with plate.

....

NOTE: For our cookbook we used an assortment of dried fruits and nuts for this Upside-down Cake.

Lemon Delicious Pudding

We don't make puddings like this very often, only once in a while when the weather turns cold and miserable. This pudding cheers the soul.

Serves 6

½ cup self-raising flour

1 cup sugar

grated rind 1 large lemon

4 tablespoons fresh lemon juice

4 tablespoons melted butter

3 large eggs, at room temperature and separated

1½ cups milk

Put the flour, sugar and lemon rind into a basin. Add lemon juice, melted butter and egg yolks.

Beat until thoroughly mixed, then stir in the milk gradually. Beat egg whites in a separate bowl until they are stiff and white. Gradually pour the lemon batter into the beaten egg whites, folding through lightly. Pour immediately into a well-buttered oven-proof dish (should be about 6 or 7 cm deep so that the pudding can separate into a fluffy cake on top and the lemon sauce underneath).

Stand the dish in a baking dish of cold water and bake in a moderate 180°C oven for about 1 hour. Cover the dish loosely with foil during the last ten minutes, if the pudding is browning too much. Serve warm with cream or vanilla ice cream.

Upside-down Cake

Dead Easy Chilli

Believe it or not, this is one of the most requested recipes I have published.

The ease and simplicity of this recipe makes it popular with everyone from children at camp to a busy mother wanting a quick and easy dinner for a growing family.

4-6 servings

600 g lean mince
2 cloves garlic
440 g can tomato soup
425 g can chilli beans (red kidney beans in mild chilli sauce)
1 green capsicum, sliced thinly (optional)

You can cook the mince, capsicum, and garlic in a little oil on the stove top till the mince changes colour. Or do the same in the microwave but without the oil, making sure the mince is stirred from time to time to avoid lumps. Add the soup and chilli beans and simmer or microwave on low. (I gave my chilli 60 mins on low setting in the microwave.)

In the microwave at full volume, the chilli beans will break up. So if time is critical, cook the mince in the microwave first without the oil, but add the capsicum and garlic. Add the soup, cover the dish and cook on high for 10 minutes. Stir, add the beans, give it another few minutes and it's ready!

Serve with grated cheese, a little light sour cream, a bottle of Tabasco, plenty of rice and a simple green salad.

Easy Beef Supper

This one-pot meal was a family favourite when we were growing up in Tauranga. After a glorious day at the beach, this savoury meal can be quickly cooked and consumed with ease.

1 cup onions, chopped
1 clove garlic, crushed
3 tablespoons butter
500 g good quality steak mince
1 tablespoon curry powder
2 potatoes, diced small
1 cup frozen peas, broken apart
2 tomatoes, diced
1½ teaspoons salt

Sauté the onions and garlic in butter until the onions are translucent. Add the steak mince and brown well. Stir in the rest of the ingredients and simmer covered for 25 minutes.

....

NOTE: This recipe works well in an electric frypan and is great for the bach after a day outdoors. Serve with salads.

Easy Beef Supper

Asian Barbecued Leg of Lamb

1 boned leg of lamb (ask the butcher to bone and butterfly the meat for you)

Place the lamb in a large plastic bag with:

½ cup malt vinegar

½ cup soy sauce

4-5 cloves garlic, finely chopped

4 tablespoons brown sugar

4 tablespoons sesame oil

4 teaspoons sweet Thai chilli sauce

ground black pepper

chopped coriander

3 teaspoons fresh ginger, sliced finely

Seal and leave for 2 days in the fridge. To prepare, cover with foil and barbecue 20 minutes on each side. You can use a pot to weight the meat down so that it cooks evenly. Serve with warm gourmet potato salad with a mint vinaigrette or baked potatoes with a little light sour cream and topped with mint or coriander pesto.

Coriander Pesto

1½ cups fresh coriander

2 cloves garlic

¼ cup freshly grated Parmesan

3 tablespoons pine nuts

5 tablespoons olive oil

salt and pepper

Combine the coriander, garlic, Parmesan and pine nuts in food processor or blender. Drizzle in the oil. Season.

French Roast Lamb

2½-3 kg leg of lamb

2 large cloves garlic

75 g French mustard

1 tablespoon rosemary

½ tsp ground ginger

2 tablespoons Worcestershire sauce

1 tablespoon olive oil

Crush the garlic and mix well with the mustard, herbs, ginger and Worcester Sauce. Slowly add the olive oil, stirring constantly, until it's a thick paste. Brush over lamb and bake at 180°C for approximately 2 hours to 2 hours 20 minutes.

Pantry Classics

Having a well-stocked pantry is a real bonus for a busy cook.

Homemade relishes, mustards, chutneys, sauces, jams and spreads make for delicious taste pointers for every meal, and they can transform a simple association – like bread and cheese – into a memorable flavour combination.

The Mediterranean table has brought pesto and tapenade into our kitchens and helped us keep simple food versatile and dynamic. For example, if the menu for dinner is chicken, potatoes and salad, adding pesto under the chicken skin and wrapping the chicken in bacon will produce a fast and delicious family meal with a special touch.

Pesto is the Italian word for paste – a thick uncooked sauce traditionally made from blending basil, garlic, pine nuts and Parmesan cheese together. Other herbs like coriander, sorrel and mint also make great pesto.

Serving suggestions for Basil Pesto:
- Add to soups like minestrone or tomato
- Use as a sandwich spread with either tuna or chicken and salad
- Top sliced tomatoes with pesto and fresh mozzarella cheese
- Add pesto to ground veal or beef when you make your next meat loaf
- Blend a little butter with pesto and serve with grilled fish
- Add a few tablespoons of pesto to your favourite stew, to a baked potato with sour cream, or spread onto a cooked pizza base as a delicious snack.
- Add a generous spoonful to a bowl of cooked pasta, or add to your favourite vinaigrette to be served with grilled vegetables and goat's cheese

Basil Pesto

$1/2$ cup pine nuts
4 cloves garlic, peeled
2 cups fresh basil leaves
$1/2$ – $2/3$ cup grated Parmesan cheese
about $1/2$ cup olive oil
salt and pepper

Toast the pine nuts briefly in a hot, dry pan until they turn golden. This only takes a few minutes, so watch them carefully as they burn easily.

Place the garlic, basil, pine nuts and Parmesan cheese in the food processor. Blend and add the oil slowly, in a thin stream until mixture is smooth. Season. Cover with a thin layer of additional oil, place in a covered, airtight, clean jar and store in the fridge for up to 2-4 weeks.

Tapenade with Sun-dried tomatoes

Tapenade is an intensely flavoured olive paste made with anchovies and capers. A jar in the fridge is a great help to the home cook. Over the years, my exposure to tapenade with sun-dried tomatoes has always been a positive experience – so now I include sun-dried tomatoes in my tapenades.

Tapenade

1 cup black olives, pitted
2-3 anchovy fillets
1 tablespoon capers, chopped and rinsed
a good squeeze of lemon juice
4 tablespoons olive oil
2 tablespoons chopped parsley
2 tablespoons sun-dried tomatoes, finely chopped
freshly ground black pepper

Put the olives, anchovies, capers, lemon juice and oil in a food processor and mix to a coarse purée.

Stir in parsley and sun-dried tomatoes, and add pepper. Add a little more olive oil if desired. Store in an airtight jar in the fridge for up to a month.

Variation: You can add a little garlic or chilli or a few chopped basil leaves to this recipe if desired.

Tapenade serving suggestions:
- Use as a base on a pizza, add to mayonnaise and serve over cold meat, or use like pesto under the skin of a chicken breast
- Toss a spoonful of tapenade through cooked, drained pasta
- Serve in a small ramekin on a large platter with crusty breads and other antipasti selections

Pear Chutney

1.3 kg firm-ripe pears

3 cloves garlic, minced

2 teaspoons salt

1 teaspoon cayenne pepper
  (or to taste)

2 teaspoons ground coriander

1 cup vinegar

a squeeze of lime or lemon juice

1$\frac{1}{2}$ cups raisins

1 tablespoon fresh ginger
  root, minced

1 cup brown sugar

$\frac{1}{2}$ cup water, if needed

Core, chop but do not peel the pears. Place in a large saucepan. (I use my stainless steel stockpot.) Add all the remaining ingredients except for the brown sugar and the water. When the pears are tender, stir in the brown sugar. If the chutney appears too thick, add the water. Then cook it down slowly for 10-20 minutes, stirring occasionally, until it has thickened. Put into hot, sterilised jars and seal when cold. Keep in a cool place and do not open for a few weeks.

● I prefer to fill one large jar and keep in the fridge and to give my other jars away for people to keep in their fridges.

Bread and Butter Pickles

8 cups sliced cucumbers or
  large gherkins

4 onions

4 capsicums, mixed red, green
  and yellow

1 cup salt

2 litres cold water

2 cups of white vinegar

2 cups sugar

2 teaspoons yellow mustard seeds

1 teaspoon pickling spice

2 teaspoons turmeric

2 teaspoons celery seed

$\frac{1}{4}$ teaspoon cinnamon

Place the cucumbers in a large, non-metallic bowl. Peel and slice the onions. Deseed and slice the capsicums. Add onions and capsicums to the cucumbers. Sprinkle over the salt and add the cold water. Leave to stand for three hours. Drain, but do not rinse. Mix the vinegar, sugar, mustard seeds, pickling spice, turmeric, celery seed and cinnamon together. Bring to the boil. Add vegetables. Bring to the boil. Simmer for one minute. Pack into hot, clean, dry jars. Seal with non-metallic lids.

Apricot Conserve

Whenever I have a supply of fresh apricots, I make this conserve. It has less sugar than a regular jam and therefore, it is not as firm. It's kept in the fridge and extra jars are given away to friends. It's best consumed within the next few weeks after it's made – but "fridge life" has never been a problem. Delicious on toast, muffins, crumpets, waffles, pancakes and to top ice cream.

1 kg apricots

juice of $\frac{1}{2}$ lemon

$\frac{1}{2}$ cup water

750 g sugar

Wash and slice the apricots, place in a large saucepan with lemon juice and water. When this mixture is hot, slowly add the sugar and stir well until the sugar dissolves. Boil gently for 15-20 minutes until apricots have cooked down and the mixture has thickened. Due to the small amount of water addded to the mixture and the short cooking time, stirring the jam will prevent the fruit mixture from jelling. Pour into hot, clean, dry jars. Seal when cold and store in the fridge.

● This is not a traditional jam, where the quantities of fruit and sugar are usually equal and the cooking time is extended so the jam passes a setting test before it is poured into jars. However, this method produces such an intense, delightful, fresh-apricot flavour, it's well worth trying!

Acknowledgements

Firstly, a huge thanks to the team that helped produce this book: chef/food stylist Rodney Greaves, stylist/location director John Borwick, assistant chef David Lilley and photographer, Kieran Scott. It is a pleasure to work with Kieran. Not only does Kieran create a memorable, artistically-appointed shot, but his ease, integrity and professionalism are exemplary.

Many thanks to Lori Schuda for cheerfully giving up weekends to help with production, to Lloyd Anderson for his advice and encouragement, to my father, John White, for his untiring support and assistance, to Jennifer Kelly for great aprons, Karl Van Den Brink of Chubby Chickens for superb product, to Corbans Wines for great vino and to Pandoro Bakery in Parnell for superb breads.

Special thanks to Cliff Josephs, Pamela Parsons and Sue Attwood for their patience and fine efforts.

Finally, to Gourmet Direct, and in particular to Jenny Myers for her expert help and assistance in sourcing and sending the best possible products for us to use in this book.

Special thanks to all our families and friends, who understood and supported this venture. In particular, one more deep and heartfelt thanks to you John, for insisting on creating something truly beautiful. Your vision, eye-to-detail and enthusiastic, positive energy made this such a fun project. Also to Rodney, for all the 6:00 a.m. starts, cups of hot coffee, shared re-testing and all your support – thank you.

When we finished the photography for this book, and when all the busy demands of producing a special cook book were behind us, we found that we all missed the laughter and camaraderie. I'm so glad that this book remains as a reminder of the wonderful and special time we all shared.

**From left to right:
John Borwick, Annabelle White,
Rodney Greaves and David Lilley**

Weights and Measures

As most cooks do not have scales in their kitchen,
where possible we have indicated measurements in cups and tablespoons.
Cup measures are loosely filled except for brown sugar, which is firmly packed.
Butter is presented in grams.

In New Zealand, South Africa, the USA and in England
1 tablespoon equals 15 ml. In Australia, 1 tablespoon equals 20 ml.
These variations will not adversely affect the end result, as long as the same spoon
is used consistently, so the proportions are correct.

Grams to Ounces and vice versa

General	Exact
30 g = 1 oz	1 oz = 28.35 g
60 g = 2 oz	2 oz = 56.70 g
90 g = 3 oz	3 oz = 85.05 g
120 g = 4 oz	4 oz = 113.04 g
150 g = 5 oz	5 oz = 141.08 g
180 g = 6 oz	6 oz = 170.01 g
210 g = 7 oz	7 oz = 198.04g
230 g = 8 oz	8 oz = 226.08 g
260 g = 9 oz	9 oz = 255.01 g
290 g = 10 oz	10 oz = 283.05 g
320 g = 11 oz	11 oz = 311.08 g
350 g = 12 oz	12 oz = 340.02 g
380 g = 13 oz	13 oz = 368.05 g
410 g = 14 oz	14 oz = 396.09 g
440 g = 15 oz	15 oz = 425.02 g
470 g = 16 oz	16 oz = 453.06 g

Recipes based on these (International Units) rounded values

Liquid Measurements

25 ml	(28.4 ml)	=1 fl oz		
150 ml	(142 ml)	=5 fl oz	= $\frac{1}{4}$ pint	= 1 gill
275 ml	(284 ml)	=10 fl oz	= $\frac{1}{2}$ pint	
425 ml	(426 ml)	=15 f1 oz	= $\frac{3}{4}$ pint	
575 ml	(568 ml)	=20 fl oz	= 1 pint	

Spoon Measures

$\frac{1}{4}$ teaspoon = 1.25 ml
$\frac{1}{2}$ teaspoon = 2.5 ml
1 teaspoon = 5 ml
1 tablespoon = 15 ml

In NZ, SA, USA and UK 1 tablespoon = 15ml.
In Australia 1 tablespoon = 20ml.

Measurements
cm to approx inches

0.5 cm = $\frac{1}{4}$"		5 cm = 2"	
1.25 cm = $\frac{1}{2}$"		7.5 cm = 3"	
2.5 cm = 1"		10 cm = 4"	

Cake Tin Sizes
cm to approx inches

15 cm = 6 "	23 cm = 9 "
18 cm = 7 "	25 cm = 10 "
20 cm = 8 "	

Alternative Names

cake tin	cake/baking pan
capsicum	sweet bell pepper
coriander	cilantro
cornflour	cornstarch
eggplant	aubergine
essence	extract
frypan	skillet
grill	broil
hard-boiled egg	hard-cooked egg
icing sugar	confectioner's sugar
king prawns	jumbo shrimps/scampi
kumara	sweet potato
minced meat	ground meat
pawpaw	papaya
rock melon	cantaloupe
seed	pip
spring onion	scallion/green onion
zucchini	courgette

Oven Temperatures
Celsius to Fahrenheit

110°C	225°F	very cool
130°C	250°F	
140°C	275°F	cool
150°C	300°F	
170°C	325°F	warm
180°C	350°F	moderate
190°C	375°F	fairly hot
200°C	400°F	
220°C	425°F	hot
230°C	450°F	very hot
240°C	475°F	

Abbreviations

g	grams		
kg	kilogram		
mm	millimetre		
cm	centimetre		
ml	millilitre		
°C	degrees celsius		
°F	degrees Farenheit		

American-Imperial

in	inch
lb	pound
oz	ounce

Index

Index